DATE DUE

THE CAUSES
OF
WORLD WAR THREE

BY C. WRIGHT MILLS

GREENWOOD PRESS, PUBLISHERS
WESTPORT, CONNECTICUT

Library of Congress Cataloging in Publication Data

Mills, Charles Wright.
    The causes of World War Three.

    "Presented in barest outline during March 1958 in
Washington, D. C., as the Sidney Hillman award lectures
at Howard University."
    Reprint of the ed. published by Simon and Schuster,
New York.
    1. United States--Foreign relations--1953-1961.
2. World politics--1955-1965. 3. United States--
Military policy. 4. Disarmament. I. Title.
[JX1417.M54 1976]   327'.172   75-31436
ISBN 0-8371-8513-0

Originally published in 1958 by Simon and Schuster,
New York.

Reprinted with the permission of Simon & Schuster, Inc.

Reprinted in 1976 by Greenwood Press,
A division of Congressional Information Service, Inc.
88 Post Road West, Westport, Connecticut 06881

Library of Congress catalog card number 75-31436
ISBN 0-8371-8513-0

Printed in the United States of America

10 9 8 7 6 5 4 3 2

FOR KATIE

CONTENTS

THE CAUSES

OF

WORLD WAR THREE

1—WAR BECOMES TOTAL—
AND ABSURD

To REFLECT upon war is to reflect upon the human condition, for that condition is now most clearly revealed by the way in which World War III is coming about. The preparations for this war are now pivotal features of the leading societies of the world. The expectation of it follows from the official definitions of world reality. In accordance with these definitions power elites decide and fail to decide; publics and masses fatalistically accept; intellectuals elaborate and justify. The drift and the thrust toward World War III is now part of the contemporary sensibility—and a defining characteristic of our epoch.

Most of the causes of World War III are accepted as "necessity"; to expect its coming is considered "realism." Politicians and journalists, intellectuals and generals, businessmen and preachers now fight this war—and busily create the historical situation in which it is viewed as inevitable. For them, "necessity" and "realism" have become ways to hide their own lack of moral and political imagination. Among the led and among the leaders moral insensibility to violence is as evident as is the readiness to practice violence. The ethos of war is now pervasive. All social and personal life is being organized in its terms. It dominates the curious spiritual life of the peoples of Christiandom. It shapes their scientific endeavor, limits their intellectual effort, swells the national budgets of the world, and has replaced what was once called diplomacy. The drive toward war is massive, subtle, official, and self-directed. War is no longer an interruption of peace; in our time, peace itself has become an uneasy interlude between wars; peace has become a perilous balance of mutual terror and mutual fright.

I.

ONCE UPON a time—perhaps even as late as World War II— "war or peace" was a reasonable choice. The cost of a war could be balanced against its possible results. The total war of absolute weapons has ended the reasonableness of this choice.

The question of strategic targets is now obsolete: World regions are the targets.

The distinction between military and civilian is obsolete: World populations are the bemused combatants.

The distinction between attack and defense is obsolete: The only defense is total attack, and "Civil Defense"—even as war propaganda—is properly regarded as a farce.

The distinction between strategic and tactical weapons is

now obsolete: Its continued use is based on ignorance of the dialectic of men at war and of the absolute meaning of the new weaponry. All purely military strategy must now reasonably be expected to end in mutual annihilation.

Military expertise as such has become irrelevant: All the problems of war and peace have now become political and moral problems.

War is no longer "a continuation of politics by other means." No political aims can be achieved by means of total war. No truly "national interests" of any nation can be served by it. No agenda that reasonable men can "believe in" makes the preparation for war sensible or promises to achieve peace in the world.

For the first time in American history, men in authority talk about an "emergency" without a foreseeable end. For the first time in world history, men find themselves preparing for a war which, they admit among themselves, none of the combatants could win. They have no image of what "victory" might mean, and no idea of any road to victory. In World War II, war aims became "unconditional"—which is to say, politically and economically empty. Yet in that war there were still strategic plans for "victory" by violent means. But for World War III there are no theories even of military victory. There are no terms of surrender and there is no confidence in the military means of imposing any such terms.

Yet men of power, even as they talk about peace, practice for war. Each side claims to be driven by the needs of self-defense, by noble intentions, by fear of the ignoble aggression of the other. Having moved to dominate Eastern Europe, the U.S.S.R. confronts U. S. bomber bases encircling the Soviet-China mainland. Having got hold of truly fearful means of violence, both antagonists are busy frightening one another, and themselves as well. Having seized control of man's relation to nature, both are turning nature's violent potential to the end of total destruction. What one side considers a defense the other considers a threat. In the vortex of the struggle, each is trapped by his own fearful outlook and by his fear of the other; each moves and is moved within a circle both vicious and lethal.

The position amounts to this: We are at the very end of the military road. It leads nowhere but to death. With war, all nations will fall. Yet the preparation of World War III is the most strenuous and massive effort of the leading societies of the world today. War has become total. And war has become absurd.

II.

U. S. FOREIGN policy is now firmly a part of this absurd condition. It has been more a set of laggard reactions than a series of imaginative responses to changing world conditions. This policy has assumed Western military superiority, at first and specifically because of the A-bomb; when that proved illusory, the H-bomb offered a short-lived hope. And always there was the smug notion that it was upon the work of Red spies in America that Soviet science was proceeding; and also, of course, that it was really the captured German scientists who were at the bottom of it all. The collapse of all these illusions did not upset the doctrinaire assumption: In the manner of all dogma, it was merely turned into General Fact. By hook or by crook the assumption was clung to: the West is superior; the Soviet system is backward; the U.S.S.R. will remain a second-rate industrial power.

Moreover, just as the Russian elite has felt that the United States would somehow collapse in economic ruin, the United

States elite has clung to the view that the Soviet system is always politically tottering. "They are in a very bad way," said Mr. Dulles to The Senate Foreign Relations Committee, six months before Sputnik I. In the end, it has been hopefully assumed, *they* will have to seek peace; then Washington will serve on Moscow its ultimatum, the terms of which nobody knows. That has been the big dream behind it all—the containment by military encirclement, the fake promises of "liberating the satellites of Eastern Europe," the invasion of Lebanon, the stupidity of supporting the puppet regime on Formosa, and the rest of it.

United States policy is still based on some such official definitions of what it is reasonable to expect. It is held that if the U. S. cannot "catch up with and overtake"—to use a well-known phrase—the Soviet missile lead, the alternatives will be: Capitulation or Extermination. In short, neither the United States nor the West generally has accepted as quite real, or legitimate, the *fact* of Soviet communism; the possibility of "peaceful coexistence" has been, and is, defined as mere Red propaganda. And toward the new beginnings in the Soviet bloc since the death of Stalin, U. S. policy has been inert and monolithic.

The doctrine of violence, and the inept opportunism based upon it, are substitutes for political and economic programs. That doctrine has been and is the fundamental basis of U. S. policy. And U. S. policy is now bankrupt. It has failed to hold back the increased influence of the Soviet Union since the end of World War II. In the nationalist terms of gain and loss, it has "lost" China and is well on the way to "losing" the Middle East, India, and much of the rest of the underdeveloped world. It has led to ever greater suspicions among noncapitalist peoples and elites, and to loss of confidence among capitalist brothers. It has become part of the moral debasement of the meaning of "Americanism" at home and abroad. It has increased the insecurity of the United States and of the world at large.

The doctrine of Massive Retaliation has become massive nonsense. Yet it is clung to rigidly, if only because official types of men have no other doctrine to which to cling. They have no image at once official and reasonable of what peace might be; they have no idea of how the kind of war they are preparing might be a means to the kind of peace they might want.

In all this, Democrats cannot point to Republicans as failures. Acheson and Dulles are in continuity; bipartisan foreign policy has become bipartisan default of policy. It is not pacifists but realists, not theorists but practical men of affairs who have been in charge of the crises men now fail to confront in this time of war's absurdity.

It is out of such elite default and incompetence that theories of historical inevitability are now constructed; it is upon such defaults that feelings of fatalistic resignation rest. But the truth, I am going to argue, is that it is the rigidity of those who have access to the new means of history-making that has created and is creating the "inevitability" of World War III. Increasingly now it becomes clear that not "fate" but doctrinaire incompetence is leading mankind into the great trap. Ours is not so much a time of big decisions as a time for big decisions that are not being made. A lot of bad little decisions are crippling the chances for the appropriate big ones.

III.

SURELY WAR and peace are now the most important issues men anywhere can reason about. Yet so total is their sense of bewilderment that, like quarreling children, their reasoning is often reduced to mere assertion and counterassertion. The arguments of leading intellectual circles about war and peace often seem merely another turn in the cold-war rhetoric that now passes in East, in West, and in between for public discourse. They are without orientation to considered values and without the guidance of clarifying definition.

Many scholars say—and many more feel—that only a fool would now publicly discuss the causes of war and the roads to peace. They believe that the human mind cannot grapple successfully with the total and ultimate issues involved, that any inquiry not more "specialized" is bound to be inadequate. Yet many, perhaps in fear of being thought Unpatriotic, become nationalist propagandists; others, perhaps in fear of being thought Unscientific, become nationalist technicians. Neither type seems able to transcend the official terms in which the world encounter is now defined. As propagandists, they are no more enlightening than any other propagandists; as technicians, they are committed in advance to some one or another narrow range of policy which they would elaborate and justify. As a result, such knowledge and skill as many students of man and society have are largely wasted so far as the human problems of war and peace are concerned.

Yet all significant problems of contemporary man and society bear upon the issues of war and peace, and the solution to any significant problem in some part rests upon their outcome. I do not believe that these issues are now as dreadfully complicated as everyone so readily tends to assume. But regardless of that, it is precisely the task of the intellectual, the scholar, the student, to confront complications; to sort out insistent issues in such a way as to open them up for the work of reason—and so for action at strategic points of intervention. It is our task continually to make the new beginning.

The epoch in which we stand is pivotal; the tradition of classic social analysis is clear. We must respond to events; we must define orienting policies. Should we fail to do so we stand in default of our intellectual and of our public duties; we abdicate such role as reason may have in human affairs. And this we should be unwilling to do.

In this exploratory essay I want to find out how, within the history of our immediate epoch, World War III is coming about. I also want to determine whether or not any identifiable group of men and women can do anything about it and, if so, who they are and what they must do if there is to be peace. I address myself neither to power elites nor to people in general, but to those who are generally aware of what is going on, who have thought about the preparation of World War III and who are becoming uneasy about it. It is my hope that their uneasiness can be turned into bolder reflection; it is my aim to help them make this turn.

In Part One I shall confront the question, "Do Men Make History?"—defining the problems of history-making—and so of war-making—for our time, examining the ideas of history as fate and of history as decision, and reassessing the idea of political responsibility.

In Part Two, I shall consider the causes of "World War III," trying to sort out from the blind drift such explicit decisions and lack of decisions as are involved.

In Part Three I shall ask, "What, Then, Ought We to Do?" To answer this question in a relevant way requires that I examine the controversial meaning of peace, state the obstacles to any program for peace, and suggest just who is in a position to do what.

In Part Four, "The Role of the Intellectuals," I shall turn to the relations of decision-makers and intellectuals and suggest specific activities to intellectuals, scientists, and ministers which they can and which they ought now to undertake.

PART ONE—DO MEN

MAKE HISTORY?

2—ON FATE AND DECISION

In what sense may it be said that men make history, and in what sense, if in any, are historical events, such as war, inevitable? Some believe that events are overwhelming; that men are trapped by circumstances, even if circumstances are in some collective way made by men. But others stress the causal role of explicit decisions in the making of history. For them, events are not overwhelming; events are themselves shapable —and often shaped—by the deliberate decisions of identifiable circles of men.

To the question of fate and decision, I think we cannot give one answer that holds for all of human history. To argue about history-making in general is to throw away our chance to understand the history-making of any given epoch. It is less useful, for example, to argue about the causes of war in general or the causes of any previous war than about what is now causing World War III. For to know the causes of the First or of the Second World War is not necessarily to know much about those of the Third. The guide rule for adequate social analysis, especially today, is that we cannot merely assume that there are Forces independent of the structure of a given epoch that are acting upon History or that if there were we could grasp them. Neither can we assume that "War" is a unitary phenomenon, always caused by uniform forces and decisions. We can best understand the causes of World War III not by studying history as the recorded past but by examining, in Paul Sweezey's phrase, "the present as history." Every epoch has its own kinds of history-making—and its own forms of war and peace, and of the conditions that lie between the two. The causes of war and the conditions of peace must be considered as historically specific to a given epoch.

So we must rephrase our question: Is war, today, a matter of blind drift, of overwhelming events, of historical destiny? Or is it a matter of men making decisions, and if so, which men?

The notion of fate is at the bottom of all notions of history as beyond human decision. In medieval Europe the ancient Greek idea of fate was transformed into the Will of God; if this Will prevails, then public events and private lives are seen as the realization of God's Big Plan—which runs for longer than five years. This idea of God as the Totalitarian Planner, I suppose, came about when nature was overwhelming: it is a preindustrial idea. As a definition of fate today it is obsolete, to say the least.

But there is another conception of fate, one that is not obsolete. A sociological idea of great and direct political use, it is in fact indispensable for adequate reflection on human affairs:

To say that a historical event is caused by fate is to say that it is the summary and unintended result of innumerable decisions of innumerable men. These men are not socially compact enough to be identifiable, and such decisions as each of them makes are not in themselves consequential enough for the results to have been foreseen. Each decision that each man makes is one among many, and the results of each decision are minute. All these decisions—coinciding, colliding, coalescing—add up to the blind result: the historical event, which, as it were, is autonomous. There is no link between any one man's intention and the summary result of the innumerable intentions. Thus, in the classic model of the capitalist market, innumerable entrepreneurs and innumerable consumers by ten thousand decisions per minute shape and reshape, in the longer run, the structure of the economy. And in like manner, the causes of such historical events as war are not under human control. Events are beyond explicit human decision.

This is the principal limitation Karl Marx had in mind when he wrote in *The Eighteenth Brumaire:* "Men make their own history, but they do not make it just as they please. They do not make it under circumstances chosen by themselves. . . ." Engels wrote in the same vein, and Tolstoy's view is similar.

This sociological conception of fate, in brief, has to do with events in history that are beyond the control of any circles or groups of men (1) compact enough to be identifiable, (2) powerful enough to decide with consequence, and (3) in a position to foresee the consequences and so to be held accountable for historical events.

So understood, fate is not a universal constant rooted in God, in Nature, or inherent in The Nature of Man or in The Nature of History.

Fate is a feature of specific kinds of social structure; the extent to which the mechanics of fate are the mechanics of history-making is itself a historical problem. How large the role of fate may be, in contrast with the role of explicit decision, depends first of all upon the scope and the concentration of the means of power that are available at any given time in any given society.

Power has to do with whatever decisions men make about the arrangements under which they live and about the events which make up the history of their times. Events that are beyond human decisions do happen; social arrangements do change without benefit of explicit decision. But insofar as such decisions are made—and insofar as they could be but are not made—the problem of who is involved in making them—or in not making them—is the basic problem of power. It is also the problem of history-making, and so of the causes of war.

The relevant means of power now include the facilities of industrial production and of military violence, of political administration and of the manipulation of opinion. According to the reach, the centralization, and the availability of such means of power, we must determine the roles of explicit decision and the mechanics of fate in the making of history.

In those societies in which the means of power are rudimentary and decentralized, history *is* fate. The innumerable actions of innumerable men modify their local milieus, and thus gradually modify the structure as a whole. These modifications—the course of history—go on behind men's backs. History is drift, although in total "men make it."

But in those societies in which the means of power are enormous in scope and centralized in form a few men may be so placed within the historical structure that by their decisions about the use of these means they modify the structural conditions under which most men live. Nowadays such elites of power make history "under circumstances not chosen altogether by themselves," yet compared with other men, and with other periods of human history, these circumstances do indeed seem less overwhelming.

I am contending that "men are free to make history" and that some men are now much freer than others to do so, for such freedom requires access to the means of decision and of power by which history can now be made. To assume that men are equally free to make history is to assume that they are equal in power. But power is a hierarchy; the shape of that hierarchy is itself subject to historical change, and at any given moment of history it opens to different men different opportunities to exercise their wills in the making of history. What to powerless men is an overwhelming event, to men of power is a decision to be made or an abdication to commit. It is a challenge, an obstacle, an opportunity, a struggle, a fear, a hope. In our time if men do not make history, they tend increasingly to become the utensils of history-makers and the mere objects of history-making. But those who do have access to the new means of power, and yet define their situation as one of fate—do they not stand now in objective default?

3—HISTORY-MAKING

IS CENTRALIZED

THE HISTORY of modern society may most readily be understood as the story of the enlargement and the centralization of the means of power. In feudal societies, these means are decentralized; in the modern age they have become centralized. The rise of industrial society has involved the development and the centralization of the means of economic production, as peasants and artisans are replaced by private corporations and government industries. The rise of the nation-state has involved similar developments in the means of violence and political administration, as kings control nobles and self-equipped knights are replaced by standing armies and military machines. The climax of all three developments—in economics, politics, and in violence—is now occurring in most dramatic form in the U.S.A. and in the U.S.S.R.

Before World War II several nations made international history; when that was the case, war was easier to explain as the blind result of their fatal interplay. But now when there are only two—and everything between them is practically a political vacuum—the making of history is more centralized and more open to the politics of explicit decision.

In the two superstates the history-making means of power are now organized. Their facilities of violence are absolute; their economic systems are increasingly autarchic; politically, each of them is increasingly a closed world; and in all these spheres their bureaucracies are world-wide. These two continental behemoths of our epoch have gone "beyond nationalism" to become the centers of blocs of previously sovereign power. They have relegated the European scatter of nations to subsidiary importance; they control the pace, and even the possibility, of industrial development among the underdeveloped peoples of the world. International power, in short, has been centralized.

In the capitalistic societies the enlargement and the coordination of the means of power have occurred gradually and many cultural traditions have restrained and shaped them. In the communist societies such developments have happened very rapidly indeed, generally without the great discourse of Western civilization, without the Renaissance and without the Reformation, and without the classic bourgeois epoch, which so greatly strengthened and gave political focus to the idea of freedom. In those societies the consolidation of power has occurred more brutally and, from the beginning, under tightly centralized authority. But in both types the means of power have now become international in scope and similar in form.

To be sure, each type has its own ups and downs; neither is as yet absolute; how they are run differs profoundly. Yet these two world-dominant societies are becoming overdeveloped in a similar way; the very terms of their world antagonism are furthering their convergence. So different are they in historical outline that in their encounter we witness the confrontation of two epochs, marked off by two kinds of revolution; yet so similar are the bureaucratic facts of their industrialization, in the context of total war, that in their encounter we also witness their parallel development.

Technically and geographically both are supernations. Unlike the societies of Europe, each has amalgamated on a continental domain a great variety of peoples and cultures. Each has expanded mightily in territory and in power. The American expansion—from a few colonies along the Atlantic seaboard to a continental domain having military outposts in half the world's nations—is no less a part of the world condition today than is the Soviet expansion.

The key to the power of both is technological development. The "materialism" of the Soviet is no more important a spiritual fact than the "materialism" of the West—especially of the U.S.A., in which religion itself is now a quite secular activity. In both, the means of production are so arranged that, in the name of efficiency, work is alienated; in both, as well, the means of consumption are culturally exploitative. In neither is there significant craftsmanship in work or significant leisure in the nonworking life. In both, men at leisure and at work are subjected to impersonal bureaucracies. This trend is no Bolshevik invention; it is part of the main line of Western, and especially of American, industrial and technical development.

In both, science and loyalty, industry and the national canons of excellence are in the service of the war system and of war preparations. In both, the Science Machine is made a cultural and a social fetish, rather than an instrument under continual public appraisal and control; and to the Machine's economic as well as military aspects, the organization of all life is increasingly adapted.

For both superstates, war is obsolete as a means of any policy save that of mutual annihilation, yet in both virtually all policies and actions fall within the perspective of a third world war. In both, the justification of means by "our ends," and the acceptance of "our violence" as a necessary means are the official doctrines—and not only doctrines but practices built into the official life of the nation.

In both, political struggles tend to be replaced by administrative decisions. As the standard of living of each advanced nation rises, indifference or fear—as the case may be—tend to make "the management of consent" and the regulation of political irregularities matters of administrative routine. Within both, most men are now the objects of history, adapting to structural changes with which they have little or nothing to do. Although they may be "taken into account" in varying degrees by dictators or democrats, they are not among the history-makers. Within both, history-making—and so war-making—is virtually monopolized by those who have access to the material and cultural means by which history is now powerfully being made.

That is the point of immediate importance: Small ruling circles in both superstates assume that military violence and the whole supporting ethos of an overdeveloped society geared for war are hardheaded, practical, inevitable, and realistic conceptions.

There are many other points of convergence and coincidence between these two countries, both in dream and in reality, and as the Soviet industrial complex is further enlarged the parallels will become more pronounced. In surface ideology they apparently differ; in structural trend and in official action they become increasingly alike. Not ideology but industrial and military technology, geared to total war, may well determine that the dreams of each will in due course be found in the realities of the other.

4—THE HIGH AND THE MIGHTY

AMONG American spokesmen there is little doubt that the high and the mighty of the Soviet Union make history. The Red Dictators are regularly blamed for evil historical consequences thought to be directly traceable to their decisions and designs. But in the formal democracies—especially now that things are not going so well—it is claimed that no elite makes history or is in any position to do so. The omnipotence of evil tyrants abroad and the prevalence of virtuous but impotent leaders at home are widely assumed. For in America, after all, "the people" are magically sovereign.

As we examine the United States in the middle of the twentieth century, we come upon many such inherited images which confuse our attempt to confront its present reality. That is one reason why history is the shank of any social study; we must study it if only to rid ourselves of it. In the United States such images usually have to do with the first half of the nineteenth century. At that time economic facilities were very widely dispersed and subject to little or no central authority. The state watched in the night but was without decisive voice in the day. One man meant one rifle, and the militia were without centralized orders. Such images are altogether historical.

Within the United States today three broad levels of power may now be distinguished: The top of modern America is increasingly unified and often seems willfully co-ordinated. At the top there has emerged an elite whose power probably exceeds that of any small group of men in world history, the Soviet elite possibly excepted. The middle levels are often a drifting set of stalemated forces; the middle does not link the bottom with the top. The bottom of this society is politically fragmented and, even as a passive fact, increasingly powerless; at the bottom there is emerging a mass society.

The power of decision is now seated in military, political, and economic institutions. Other institutions are increasingly shaped and used by these big three. By them the push, the drive, of a fabulous technology is now guided, even as it paces and shapes their own development. As each of the big three has assumed its modern shape, its effects upon the other two have become greater and the traffic among the three has increased. The U. S. power system is no longer composed of a self-contained economy and a self-contained political order, loosely incorporating local militia unimportant to politics and to money-making. This system is now a political economy intricately linked with a military order central to politics and crucial to money-making. The triangle of power formed by these three orders is now a structural fact, and it is the key to any understanding of the higher circles in America today.

For as each of these domains has coincided with the others, as decisions in each have become broader, the leading men of each—the high military, the corporation executives, the political directorate—have tended to come together, to form the power elite of America.

I. The political order, once composed of several dozen states with a weak federal center, has become an executive apparatus which has taken unto itself many previously scattered powers, legislative and administrative. It now reaches into all parts of the social structure. Business and government have become more closely and explicitly connected; neither can now be seen clearly as a distinct world. Under American conditions the growth of executive government does not mean merely the "enlargement of government" as some kind of autonomous bureaucracy; it means the ascendancy of the corporation men into political eminence. Already during the New Deal such men had joined the political directorate; as of World War II they came to dominate it. Long involved with government, now they have moved into full direction of the economy of the war effort and of the postwar era.

II. The economy—once a great scatter of small productive units in somewhat autonomous balance—has become internally dominated by a few hundred corporations, administratively and politically interrelated, which together hold the keys to economic decision. This economy is at once a permanent war economy and a private corporation economy. Its most important relations to the state now rest on the coincidence between military and corporate interests, as defined by generals and businessmen and accepted by politicians and public. Within the elite as a whole, this coincidence of military domain and corporate realm strengthens both of them and further subordinates the merely political man. Not the party politician but the corporation executive is now more likely to sit with military men and answer the question, "What is to be done?"

III. The military order, once a meager establishment in a context of civilian distrust, has become the largest and most expensive feature of government. Behind smiling public relations, it has all the grim and clumsy efficiency of a great and sprawling bureaucracy. The seemingly permanent military threat places a premium upon high military personnel; virtually all political and economic actions are now judged in terms of military definitions of reality. The higher military, in short, have ascended to a firm position within the power elite of our time.

In considerable part, this power elite is the result of the historical fact, pivotal for the years since 1939, that attention has shifted from domestic problems centered on slump to international problems centered on war. Nowadays even slump (not to speak of poverty) must be seen, and is seen by knowledgeable higher-ups, in its international bearing. By long historical usage the government of the United States has been shaped by purely domestic clash and balance; it does not have suitable agencies and traditions for the democratic handling of international affairs. It is in this vacuum that the power elite has grown.

The unity of this elite rests in part upon the similar psychology of its several members, but behind this kind of unity there lie those institutional hierarchies over which the political directorate, the corporate rich, and the grand military now preside. How each of these hierarchies is shaped and what relations it has with the others determine in large part the relations of their rulers. The unity of the elite is not a simple reflection of the unity of institutions, but men and institutions are always related. That is why we must understand the elite today in connection with such institutional trends as the development of a permanent war establishment, alongside a privately incorporated economy, inside a virtual political vacuum. For the men at the top have been selected and formed by such institutional trends.

Their unity, however, does not rest solely upon psychological similarity nor even upon the structural blending of commanding positions and common interests. At times it is a more explicit co-ordination. Such co-ordination is neither total nor continuous; often it is not very sure-footed. The power elite has *not* emerged as the realization of any plot. Yet we must remember that institutional trends may be defined as opportunities by those who occupy the command posts. Once such opportunities are recognized, men may avail themselves of them. Certain types of men from each of these three areas, more farsighted than others, actively promoted the liaison even before it took its truly modern shape. Now more have come to see that their several interests can more easily be realized if they work together, in informal as well as in formal ways, and accordingly they have done so.

The idea of the power elite is, of course, an interpretation. It enables us to make sense of major institutional trends, of the social similarities and psychological affinities of the men at the top, and of such explicit co-ordination as we may observe among them. But it is also based upon what has been happening on the middle and lower levels of power.

5—THE SEMIORGANIZED

STALEMATE

THE AMERICAN system of power is usually interpreted as a moving balance of many competing interests. In the nineteenth century the balance was thought to occur among a great scatter of individuals and enterprises; in the twentieth century it is thought to occur among great interest blocs. In both views the politician is the key man of power because he is the broker of many conflicting powers.

The balance and the compromise in American society—the "countervailing powers" and the numerous associations, the "veto groups" and the "vested interests"—must now be seen as having mainly to do with the *middle* levels of power. It is about these middle levels that political journalists and scholars of politics are most likely to write if only because, being mainly middle-class themselves, they are closer to them. These levels provide the noisy content of most political news and gossip; images of these levels are more or less in accord with the folklore of how democracy works; and, if the master image of balance is accepted, many intellectuals, in their current patrioteering, are readily able to satisfy such political optimism as they wish to feel. Accordingly, such liberal interpretations of what is happening in the United States are now virtually the only interpretations that are widely distributed.

But to believe that the power system reflects a balancing society is, I think, to confuse the present era with an earlier time and to confuse its top and bottom with its middle levels.

By the top levels, as distinguished from the middle, I refer, first, to the scope of the decisions that are made. At the top today those decisions have to do with all the issues of war and peace. They have also to do with slump and poverty, which are now so very much problems of international scope. I refer, secondly, to whether or not the groups that struggle politically have a chance to gain the positions from which such top decisions are made, and indeed whether their members do usually seek such top national command.

Most of the competing interests that make up the clang and clash of American politics are strictly concerned with their slice of the existing pie. Labor unions, for example, certainly have no international policies of an independent sort, other than those that given unions adopt for the strict economic protection of their members. Neither do farm organizations. The actions of such middle-level powers may indeed have consequences for top-level policy; certainly at times they hamper or facilitate these policies. But they are not truly concerned with them, which means, for one thing, that such influence as they do have often tends to be quite irresponsible.

The expanded, centralized, and interlocked hierarchies over which the power elite presides have encroached upon the old balances and relegated them to the middle level. This middle level, it seems to me, is better understood as an affair of entrenched and provincial demands than as a center of national decision.

I. Politics is not a forum in which the big decisions of national and international life are debated. Such debate is not carried on by nationally responsible parties representing and clarifying alternative policies. There are no such parties in the United States. More and more, fundamental issues never come to any point of decision before the Congress, much less before the electorate in party campaigns. In the case of the Quemoy incident, in the spring of 1955, the Congress abdicated all debate concerning events and decisions which surely bordered on war. The same is largely true of the 1958 crises in the Middle East and in the Far East. Such decisions now regularly bypass the Congress and are never clearly focused issues for public decision.

II. Free and independent organizations do not politically connect the lower and middle levels of society with the top levels of decision. Such organizations are not a decisive feature of American life today. As more people are drawn into the political realm, their associations become mass in scale and the power of the individual becomes dependent upon them; to the extent that associations are effective they have become larger, and to that extent also they have become less accessible to the influence of the individual. This is a central fact about associations in any mass society; it is of most consequence for political parties and for trade unions.

III. The idea that this society is a balance of powers requires us to assume that the units in balance are of more or less equal power and that they are truly independent of one another. These assumptions have rested, it seems clear, upon the historical importance of a large and independent middle class. In the latter nineteenth century and during the Progressive Era, such a class of farmers and small businessmen fought politically—and lost—their last struggle for a paramount role in national decisions. Even then their aspirations seemed bound to their own imagined past. This old, independent middle class has of course declined. Moreover, it has become politically as well as economically dependent upon the state, most notably in the case of the subsidized farmer.

The new middle class of white-collar employees is certainly not the political pivot of any balancing society. It is in no way politically united. Its trade unions, such as they are, often serve merely to incorporate it as a hanger-on of the labor interest. For a considerable period the old middle class was an independent base of power; the new middle class cannot be. Once political freedom and economic security were anchored in small and independent properties; they are not anchored in the worlds of the white-collar job. Once scattered property holders were economically linked by more or less free markets; the jobs of the new middle class are now integrated by corporate authority. Economically the white-collar classes are in the same condition as wage workers; politically they are in a worse condition, for they are not as organized. They are no vanguard of historic change; they are at best a rear guard of the welfare state.

The agrarian revolt of the nineties, the small-business revolt that has been more or less continuous since the eighties, the labor revolt of the thirties—each of these has failed as an independent movement which could "countervail" the powers that be. But each has succeeded, in varying degrees, as an interest vested in the expanded corporation and state; each has succeeded as a parochial interest seated in particular districts, in local divisions of the two parties, and in the Congress. What they have become, in short, are established elements of the *middle* levels of balancing power, in which we may now observe all those strata and interests which in the course of American history have been defeated in their bids for top power, or have never made such bids.

U. S. society is characterized by the increasing integration of real, and of potential, democratic forces into the expanded apparatus of the state. Much of what was once called "the invisible government" is now part of the quite visible government. The "governmentalization of the lobby" occurs in both the legislative and executive domains, as well as between them. Bureaucratic administration replaces electoral policies; the maneuvering of cliques replaces the open clash of parties. Corporation men move into the political directorate, and the decline of Congressional politicians to the middle levels of power is accelerated. The legislative function often becomes merely a balancing of sovereign localities and partial interests. A higher civil service that is a politically neutral, but politically relevant, depository of brain power and executive skill is virtually absent. Behind the increased official secrecy great decisions are made without benefit of public or even of Congressional debate.

In the U.S.S.R. and in modern totalitarianism in general the integration of autonomous forces is explicit; in the formal democracies it is much less so, and it is by no means a completed process. Yet it is well under way. Leaders of cliques, pressure groups, and associations maneuver within and between the organs of the democratic state and become a central part of that state. They discipline those whom they represent; their chief desire is to maintain their organizations, even if this requires them to lose sight of their ends in the effort to secure themselves as means, even if it results in their loss of independent action. They ensnare one another; such history as they make *is* history going on behind men's backs, including their own. The middle level of power in America is no moving balance; it is a semiorganized stalemate.

6—THE GREAT

AMERICAN PUBLIC

THE RISE of the power elite and the relegation of formal democratic machinery to the middle levels of power are paralleled by the transformation of publics in America into a mass society.

In a society of publics, discussion is the ascendant means of communication. The mass media, if they exist, simply enlarge and animate this discussion, linking one face-to-face public with the discussions of another.

In a mass society the dominant type of communication is the formal media; publics become mere markets for those media. The "public" of a radio program consists of all those exposed to it.

When we try to understand the United States today as a

society of publics, we come to realize that it has moved a considerable distance along the road to the mass society. In official life "the public" has come to have a phantom meaning. Some of those who clamor publicly on the middle levels, the dominant elites can identify as "Labor," others as "Small Business," still others as "Farmer." But these are not "the public." The public consists of the nonpartisan in a world of partisan interests; it is composed of those remnants of the old and new middle classes whose interests are not explicitly defined, organized, or clamorous. In a curious adaptation, "the public" often becomes, in administrative fact, "the disengaged expert" who, although ever so well informed, has never publically taken a clear-cut stand on controversial issues. He is the "public" member of The Board, The Commission, The Committee. What the public stands for, accordingly, is often a vagueness of policy (called "open-mindedness"), a lack of involvement in public affairs (known as "reasonableness"), and a professional disinterest (called "tolerance").

All this is indeed far removed from the eighteenth-century idea of the public of public opinion. In that classic image the people are presented with problems. They discuss them. They formulate viewpoints. These viewpoints are organized. They compete. One viewpoint wins out. Then the people act on this view, or their representatives are instructed to act it out, and this they promptly do.

Such images of democracy are still used as working justifications of power in America. Surely we must all now recognize such descriptions as more fairy tale than useful approximation. The issues that now shape man's fate are neither raised nor decided by any public at large. The idea of a society that is at bottom composed of publics and run by publics is not a matter of fact; it is the proclamation of an ideal and, as well, the assertion of a legitimation masquerading as fact.

I. As the political order is enlarged and centralized it becomes less political and more bureaucratic, less the locale of a struggle than an object to be managed.

II. The old middle classes—once an independent source of democratic strength—are transformed into a set of white-collar men who duly make their declarations of dependence.

III. Mass communications do not link and feed discussion circles; they convert them into mere media markets. They do not truly communicate; they trivialize and they distract.

IV. Communities decline; the metropolitan segregation of men and women into narrow routines and milieus causes them to lose any sense of integrity as a public that might have structural relevance for the history of their society.

V. Voluntary associations, open to individuals and small groups and connecting them with centers of power, no longer are dominant features of the social structure of the United States.

Such trends—and others like them—are well known; but they are not usually seen all together as a coinciding set of forces. When they are so viewed does it not become clear that the American people are now far less a political public than a politically indifferent—although sometimes politically entertainable—mass society? Publics, like free associations, can be deliberately and suddenly smashed, or they can more slowly wither away. But whether smashed in a week or withered in a generation, the demise of the public must be seen in connection with the rise of centralized organizations, with all their new means of power, including those of the mass media of distraction. These, we now know, often seem to expropriate the rationality and the will of the terrorized or—as the case may be—the voluntarily indifferent society of masses. In the more democratic process of indifference, the remnants of such publics as remain may only occasionally be intimidated by fanatics in search of "disloyalty." But regardless of that they lose their will for decision because they do not possess the means of decision; they lose their sense of political belonging because they do not belong; they lose their political will because they see no way to realize it.

Today we cannot merely assume that in the last resort men must always be governed by their own consent. For among the means of power that now prevail is the power to manage and to manipulate the consent of men. We do not know the limits of such power and we hope it does have limits, but these considerations do not remove the fact that much power today is successfully employed without the sanction of the reason or the conscience of the obedient.

Coercion, in the last resort, is the "final" form of power, but of course we are by no means constantly at the last resort. *Authority* (power that is justified by the beliefs of the voluntarily obedient) and *manipulation* (power that is wielded unbeknownst to the powerless) must also be considered, along with coercion. In fact, whenever we think about power, the three types must be sorted out.

In the modern world, I think, power is often not so authoritative as it seemed to be in the medieval epoch. Ideas which justify rulers, which transform power into authority, do not seem to be necessary to the exercise of considerable power today. At least for many of the great decisions of our time, mass "persuasion" has not been "necessary"; the fact is simply accomplished. Furthermore, such ideas as are available to the powerful are often neither taken up nor used by them. Justifying ideologies usually arise as a response to an effective debunking of authority; in the United States such opposition has not recently been effective enough to create the felt need for new ideologies of rule.

7—ON TRAGEDY AND
RESPONSIBILITY

THESE developments cannot be correctly understood in terms of either the liberal or the Marxian interpretation of politics and history. Each of these ways of thought arose as a guideline to reflection about a type of society which does not now exist in the United States or in the Soviet Union. In these two nations, we now confront new kinds of social structure, which embody tendencies of all modern society but in which these tendencies have assumed a more naked and flamboyant prominence, and perhaps qualitatively new forms.

That does not mean that we must give up the ideals of these classic political doctrines. I believe that both these political legacies, in their classic nineteenth-century statements, have been concerned with the problems of rationality and of freedom. In liberalism, freedom and rationality are supreme facts about the individual; in Marxism, they are supreme facts about men's role in the making of history. The ideas of freedom and of rationality, I think it evident, are now quite ambiguous in the new societies of the United States and of the Soviet Union. But I do not think that this is the only meaning of recent world history. The rise of the power elite is a token of the centralization of the means of history-making itself—and this fact opens up new opportunities for the willful making of history.

Many observers fail to recognize this implication of the new centralization of the enlarged means of power—between nations and within them; some hesitate or refuse to do so because they feel that the rise of such power elites and the institutional means of power that underpin them are too pessimistic a finding. I believe the contrary. And quite apart from that: these *are* the kinds of reality with which we must deal if we would confront the nature of history-making and perhaps take part in the making of it. I believe that these new formations of power may be viewed in an optimistic way.

The old international balance of several or of many relatively equal nation-states has been replaced by a polarized world. Before this polarization, the balance of power between nations limited the international power of any one nation's elite. Then the mechanics of international affairs were often the mechanics of fate. But now the decisive interplay is between two superstates. In the international realm, events have become less subject to fate, more subject to human decision. Given the scope and the centralization of the means of power now organized in these two superstates, the role of explicit decision is enlarged. Those who have access to these new means of history-making have become explicitly strategic in such matters as the causes of war and the perpetuation of conditions that are cumulatively leading to war.

This situation increases the weight of those causes of war which lie within nations and which influence the decisions made and the defaults committed by elites in their sovereign names. The enlargement and the centralization of the means of power is a symptom of the chance of men really to make history; it is a signal of their opportunity to transcend fate and to allow decision—and so, possibly, reason—to make a difference in the shaping of this epoch.

Surely these developments mean that if those who now occupy the new command posts are not capable of avoiding World War III, then they are legitimate and accessible targets for intellectual examination, for moral debate, and for political action. However irresponsible these elites may now seem, and may now be, their existence makes it possible, indeed necessary, to use in our analysis and demands the idea of political responsibility. For if within the structure of our historical epoch the means of power are such as to make their use or lack of use truly consequential, then the decisions about their uses become pivots of history, and those who might use them with foresight, those who decide or fail to decide, may be held responsible to other men who do not have access to these means.

If history is fate, then everybody—and hence nobody—is responsible for such events as war. Then the purpose of analysis is to do no more than reveal the mechanics of our fate. Then there can be no serious expectations of any strategy whereby human will or reason can stop the thrust toward World War III. Then men, overwhelmed by events, embroiled in circumstances, can find in history no points of intervention. Then reason becomes a sugaring of the bitter pill of political impotence, an excuse for accepting it and, in quite real effect, a justification of the status quo, and so of the drift and the thrust toward war.

But is not the idea of history as fate, after all, mere romanticism which the adolescent, in his personal and social loneliness, often finds attractive? Is it not a way of saying to oneself and to others, "We're all in this together, the butcher and the general and the ditchdigger and the Secretary of the Treasury and the cook and the President of the United States. So let's all feel sad about one another, or, if we're up to it, let's just see it all as one great comedy."

But "we" are *not* all in this together, so far as the making of such decisions as are made and can be made is concerned.

"We" *are* all in this together, so far as bearing the consequences of these decisions is concerned.

To deny either statement, I believe, is to deny the facts of power. For the comfortable college professor of some overdeveloped society to place himself tragically in the same category as the slave in Arabia or the peasant in India is surely as presumptuous as to place himself (along with the slave and the peasant) in the same tragic positions as are occupied by the President of the United States, King Saud, or the men of the changing inner circle of the Soviet Union. Only if all men everywhere were actors of equal power in an absolute democracy of power could we seriously hold the "tragic view" of responsibility.

The tragedians generalize the "we" of their lament to the generically human, and in so doing they shove it beyond the sphere of politics. But the replacement of the straightforward idea of "political accountability" by the dead-beat notion of "tragic responsibility" is not good enough. Certainly not today; certainly not in the United States today. It is merely a convenient escape from the frustrations of politics, and a grand but false view of one's own role in human affairs. It is a lugubrious and fatalistic dodge which, adorned with a little liberal rhetoric, leads directly to the political irresponsibility of the conservative default.

To believe in political responsibility is to recognize that there may be power elites who are irresponsible because of general incompetence or because they are possessed by dogmas which incapacitate them for certain uses of the power available to them. And of course it means that they may be both dogmatic and incompetent. The ready inference from the proclamations of the U. S. elite and from their decisions and lack of decisions is that this is indeed the case. This may be taken as a profoundly pessimistic fact, and certainly it is a perilous one. But it may also be recognized as a cheering condition, for do not the consequences of their very stupidity and their rigid incompetence mean that it is now possible for intelligence and vision to be relevant to the making of history? Does it not mean that the structure of power characteristic of our epoch opens the way to a greater role for reason in human affairs?

The idea of political responsibility stands opposite the idea of historical inevitability. To understand that history—in particular the history of World War III—is not inevitable is to grasp its causes as an intellectual problem and as a set of political issues, rather than in the obscure and now fearful terms of a human destiny which overwhelms good little men who are doing their best, even though it is far from good enough.

The power elite are not merely men of good will who are doing their best. They are also men of power. No doubt they are all honorable men, but what is honor? Honor can only mean living up to a code that one believes to be honorable. There is no one code upor. which all men are agreed. The question is not: Are these honorable men? The question is: What are their codes of honor? The answer is: They are the codes of their own circles; how could it be otherwise?

And the same is true of their patriotism, of their earnest desire to serve the nation as a whole. Like codes of honor, feelings of patriotism and doctrines of the nation's good are not ultimate facts. They are matters on which there exists a great variety of opinion. They are inherent in what a man has become by virtue of how and with whom he has lived, of how he has made his living and, as well, how he has made himself.

The elite cannot be truly thought of as men who are merely "doing their duty." In considerable part they are the ones who determine their duty, as well as the duties of other men. They do not merely follow orders; they give orders. They are not merely bureaucrats; they command bureaucracies. They may try to disguise these facts from others and from themselves by appealing to traditions of which they imagine themselves to be the instruments, but there are many traditions, and they must choose which ones they will serve. And now they face decisions for which there simply are no traditions.

We cannot reason about public events and historical trends merely from knowledge about the motives and characters of the men who sit in the seats of the high and mighty. But this does not mean that we should blunt our analysis because we are accused of impugning the honor, the integrity, or the ability of those who are in high office. It is not, in the first instance, a question of individual character; and if, in further instances, we find that it is, we should not hesitate to say so plainly.

In the meantime we must judge men of power by the

standards of power, by what they do and by what they fail to do as decision-makers, not by who they are or what they may do in private life. We must judge them in terms of their policies and in terms of the consequences of their conduct of office. For they are men who command the dominant institutions of a dominant nation; they are in a position to make decisions with terrible or wonderful consequences for the underlying populations of the world; and now they are within the drift and the thrust toward World War III.

Drift means that the consequences of innumerable decisions coalesce and collide to form the blind and overwhelming events of historical fate—in the present case, of war.

Thrust means, first, such fate insofar as it operates because of explicit default; and second, the explicit decisions that are making for war.

Given the general obfuscation and indecision, the hesitation and vacillation, in a word, the semiorganized irresponsibility that prevails, it is difficult to distinguish clearly drift from thrust. Both are of course at work, but as we come to understand the mechanics of history-making since World War II, I think we come to understand that there is more thrust and less drift than we had previously supposed. Of the two, thrust, I believe, is now the more important, and certainly the more strategic, consideration for those who would be at peace. True drift is not open to explicit human decision; thrust can be stopped by appropriate and powerful decision. What some commentators mistake as "the tragic sense of life" is political nonsense. To assert that by their decisions men *can* now wrest events from fate does not require us to assume some vague "conspiracy theory." And it is not "mere denunciation" to say that today when men leave their decisions to fate, as leaders, they stand irresponsibly in the human default.

PART TWO—WORLD WAR
THREE

8—THE PIVOTAL DECISION

TOMORROW morning, it is easy to suppose, the equipment of a U. S. radar man somewhere in Canada mechanically fails, or under extreme pressure of time he mistakes a dead satellite or a stray meteor for an incoming ballistic missile. He tracks it toward the industrial heart of the U.S.A. In a few minutes his alarm is out, and in a few more—about fifteen minutes in all, we are told—the planes of the Strategic Air Command, from several dozen bases tucked in as close as they can get to the U.S.S.R., zero in on Soviet industries and cities.

The "fail safe" system of orders comes into operation, but no mechanical systems are foolproof. In the balance of terror, mechanical error and human misjudgment are unknown statistical probabilities. And the danger of miscalculation increases as the weapons become greater in power, speed, and range. On either side, should a ghost electronic echo on a radar screen trigger the launching of a missile, there are—we are told of the U. S. system—only some three hundred seconds to destroy it after its launching toward its Soviet target. Moreover, as nuclear weapons are distributed to other nations the chances of accident increase. American military men, we may suppose, simply cannot make mistakes, garble radio messages, or, while on flying missions, become mentally deranged. But might not Russians be subject to such accidents? "Over the long run," Harry Lustig, a physicist, has reflected, "it does not matter how small the probability of an accident is per unit time; it is mathematically demonstrable that as time goes on, this probability approaches certainty."

Should accident or breakdown occur, SAC drops its stuff. Or the missile is launched. The Americans have massively retaliated. The Russians retaliate massively. A few hours later the world is a radioactive shambles, a chaos of disaster.

Assuming that anyone is still around and capable of curiosity, what were the causes of World War III? And was anyone responsible for it? Certainly the radar man is not; somebody else sent him there and he followed instructions as best he could. If we follow that chain of instructions we end up in such symbolic centers as Pentagon and White House and Kremlin; out of those centers, too, we follow the network of near-automatic reactions that sent SAC hurtling toward the Soviet.

Just now, the chance of a deliberately planned war is perhaps not as great as is the "accidental" precipitation of war. But the prime conditions of the "accident" are not themselves accidental; they are planned and deliberate. The war mechanism of U. S. men and machines is all set up and triggered to go. It stands opposite a similar mechanism of Soviet design and maintenance. The first cause of World War III is, obviously, the existence of these bureaucratic and lethal machineries. Without them there could be no war.

But who caused these mechanisms to be built and maintained? Certainly not "the Russian people" or "the American people." "All men" have not decided to build and maintain the machineries of the arms race; most men have not been consulted.

At the top of the military hierarchy from which the radar man received his instructions are a few hundred professional military agents. They are in charge and they set up and maintain the U. S. war machine. At the top of the industrial complex which built these machines there are several hundred corporate rich and their executives who run the key sectors of this economy. At the top of the state—to which both military men and corporation executives look—there are a few hundred political directors who, with the aid and advice of military and business elites, make ultimate decisions about the shaping and about the uses of these war machines.

All of it, of course, is "in the name of the nation," but in itself what does that mean? That is a formula of power which may or may not mean something beyond the uses of mere rhetoric. We should never forget that no nation-state is a homogeneous entity, that none is in itself a history-making agent. "It" does not possess decision or will or interest or honor or fright. "Nation" refers to a people occupying a more or less defined territory and organized under the authority of a state or, with some chance of success, claiming such an autonomous organization. The "state," a dominating apparatus, refers to an organization that effectively monopolizes the legitimate means of violence and administration over a defined territory. "Legitimate" means: more or less generally acquiesced in by publics and masses, for reasons in which they believe. In the case of the nation-state these reasons are the symbols and ideologies of nationalism. "Nation" and "state," I think, must be used mainly as adjectives referring to national spokesmen, power elites, and policy-makers. People who are not among such men form the underlying population, which is part of the historical context but which is not itself among the history-makers today.

The causes of this war are not inherent in some vague, historical context of drift and maneuver called "international relations." The causes are seated mainly in the U.S.A. and the U.S.S.R. The immediate cause of World War III is the preparation of it. The indispensable condition for this kind of preparation is the fact of the sovereign state as a continental economic domain. International events are increasingly the result of the decisions and the lack of decisions of men who act in the name of these nations and with the means of action made available by their economic, military, and political institutions. The international centralization of decision and the internal development of the superstates, we have seen, mean that history-making is less a matter of some overwhelming fate than of the decisions and the defaults of two power elites. Accordingly, the viewpoints these elites hold, the definitions of reality they accept and act upon, the policies they espouse and attempt to realize—these are among the immediate causes of the thrust toward World War III.

And in both Russia and America, the ruling circles are possessed by the military metaphysic.

Confronted by the buzzing confusion of the world in which they live, decision-makers regularly seize upon the threat of violence as "the real factor." The deciding point in the conflict between Soviet communism and American capitalism is held (especially, it now must be admitted, by the elite of the U.S.A.) to be the state of violence and the balance of fright. The pivotal decision made by the elite is in accordance with this military metaphysic. It is the decision, as Lewis Mumford has put it, of trying "to solve the problems of absolute peace, presented by nuclear weapons, by concentrating their national resources upon instruments of genocide." It rests upon the dogmatic view—held, I am sure, with sincerity and good intention—that only by accumulating ever new and ever greater military peril can a condition of peace be created. The key moral fact about it is the virtual absence within ourselves of opposition to this definition of world reality, to the elites' strategy and policies. The key political and intellectual result is the absence within Russia and within America, among publics and masses, of any truly debated alternatives.

In terms of this metaphysic of violence, elite spokesmen now regularly interchange unpleasantries; their policy-makers plan each other's ruin. Official definitions of world reality and virtually all discourse of significant public relevance are in their hands, and they are at proclamatory war. Each defines his own nation's reality in terms of his own nation's favorite proclamations; each defines the reality of the other nation in terms of its worst decisions and actions. Surely their conduct of affairs is the key instance today of what Jacob Burckhart had in mind a hundred years ago when he predicted "the age of the terrible simplifiers."

The arms race is the master line of action followed by the power elites of the continental states. It is not subordinated to and made an instrument of any economic and political goal. What is the economic and political goal of the U. S., to which its military actions are a means? The accumulation of military power has become an ascendant end in itself; economic and political maneuvers and hesitations—from imperialist action in the desert to diplomatic coyness in the drawing room—are subordinated to and judged in terms of military forces and potentials. The spokesmen of each side say they know that war is obsolete as a means of policy, yet they search for peace by warlike means. The strategic outlook is not decisively, and certainly not permanently, changed by any one or another turn of the arms race. We are beyond that. The equipment in combat readiness on both sides is already devastating. The development of this equipment is cumulative: One "ultimate weapon" follows another in geometric progression, and the base for the acceleration in both war camps is quite adequate for the end in view. Never before has there been an arms race of this sort—a scientific arms race, with a series of ultimate weapons, dominated by the strategy of obliteration. At every turn of this "competition," each side becomes more edgy and the chances become greater that accidents of character or of technology, that the U. S. radar man in Canada or his Russian counterpart in Siberia, will trigger the sudden ending.

But the strategic outlook is the idiot's outlook. It is the fact of this idiot's race that is important, not the score at any given moment, not the alarmist cries which would frighten men from examining its deadly assumptions. ("The last thing [Western statesmen] wanted," a veteran Washington correspondent said in the last weeks of October 1957, "was to deprive the Western world of its Sputnik-inspired fright . . .") Both the Russian and the American elites, and intellectuals in both societies, are fighting the cold war in the name of peace, but the assumptions of their policies and the effects of their interactions have been, and are, increasing the

chances of war. War, it is assumed in their military metaphysic, is the most likely outcome of the parallel existence
of the two types of political economy. Such is the official
lay of the land, the official definition of world reality, the
contribution to peace of the nationalist spokesmen among
the power elite.

9—THE MILITARY

METAPHYSICIANS

WHY does the U. S. power elite accept this military meta-physic? Why in its terms do they make the arms-race decisions that are now among the central causes of World War III? Why do they seem so incapable of making the political decisions that might well stop the thrust toward this war? The reasons, I think, have to do with the shape and condition of military, economic, and political institutions, and with the permissive condition into which publics and masses and intellectuals have fallen and been pushed. In this chapter I shall take up the role of military institutions and of military men.

I. The United States, we are often told, is a peace-loving nation. The historical record, however, is less clear-cut than the proclamations of the nationalist spokesmen. Perhaps all the war and violence in which the U. S. has engaged have been duly regarded as a nuisance interfering with the more important business at hand, but, at the very least, must it not be recognized that violence as a means and even as a value is just a little ambiguous in American life and culture? *

II. Regardless of the answer, we should remember how very easy a military time the United States has had—given its geographical isolation, its readily pacified domestic markets, its labor force fed by an eager immigration, its fabulous natural resources. All these requirements, and others, of industrialization and of money-making have involved military

---

* The United States has followed the slogan that "the only good Indian is a dead Indian," thus avoiding the undemocratic development of Latin America—the taking of slaves and the creation of serfs. In addition to over a century of running battles and skirmishes with Indians, since 1776 the U. S. has engaged in seven foreign wars and a four-year civil war; it has fought English, Germans, Austrians, Chinese, Mexicans, Frenchmen, Spaniards, Italians, Japanese; it has invaded without formal declarations Haiti, Mexico, China, Russia, Nicaragua, Lebanon. "It is generally supposed," the editors of *Fortune* wrote in 1935, "that the American military ideal is peace. But unfortunately for this high-school classic, the U. S. Army, since 1776, has filched more square miles of the earth by sheer military conquest than any army in the world, except only that of Great Britain. And as between Great Britain and the U. S. it has been a close race, Britain having conquered something over 3,500,000 square miles since that date, and the U. S. (if one includes wresting the Louisiana Purchase from the Indians) something over 3,100,000. The English-speaking people have done themselves proud in this regard."

But forget the past, if you wish. Today the U. S. is allied with the British, the Germans, the French, the Japanese—none of them notable for altogether peaceful histories. It arms itself mightily in order to insure peace or to be able to resist the coming Russian attack—that is why U. S. bases, now on a fifteen-minute alert, encircle so closely the Sino-Soviet bloc. Having accumulated enough explosives to eliminate life on earth, it continues to produce explosives, to search for more powerful bombs, and to create more efficient means of their delivery.

operations only against technologically primitive populations. But now for the first time in its history the power elite of America finds itself in a military neighborhood. It *is* a fearful neighborhood; and this elite is inexperienced, and frightened. Today the U. S. is much more a military neighbor of the Soviet Union than in previous centuries Germany was of France. That is the geographic meaning of the new weaponry—and a major clue to the inexperienced elite's acceptance of the military metaphysic.

III. For the first time in its history the U. S. elite definitely includes among its executives and politicians and lawyers the warlords of Washington. Historically, the professional military have been uneasy and poor relations of the elite; now they are demanding first cousins and soon, many competent observers feel, they may well become elder brothers.

Militarism has been defined by Alfred Vagts as a case of the dominance of means over ends for the purpose of heightening the prestige and increasing the power of the military. This is, of course, a conception from the standpoint of the civilian who would consider the military as strictly a means for civilian political ends. As a definition it points to the tendency of military men not to remain means but to pursue ends of their own and to turn other institutions into means for accomplishing them. In itself, the military pursuit of status is no threat of military dominance. In fact, well enclosed in the standing army, such status is a reward for military relinquishment of adventures in political power. So long as this pursuit of status is confined to the military hierarchy itself it is an important feature of military discipline and no doubt a source of much military gratification. But it becomes a threat when it is sought outside the military hierarchy and when it tends to become a basis of national policy.

Everywhere now there are the generals and the captains who, by their presence, create and maintain a militarist atmosphere. Professional economists usually consider military institutions as parasitic upon the means of economic production. Now, however, military institutions and aims have come to shape much of the economic life of the United States, without which the war machine could not exist. Religion, virtually without exception, blesses the nation at war, and recruits from among its officials the chaplain, who in military costume eases the conscience and stiffens the morale of men at war. Military men have entered political and diplomatic circles; they have gone into the higher echelons of the corporate economy; they have taken charge of scientific and technological endeavor; they have influenced higher educational institutions; they are operating a truly enormous public-relations and propaganda machinery.

iv. The rise of the warlords to enlarged command and increased status is but the most obvious sign of the fact that decisions of the greatest consequence have become largely international, and that the economics and the policies of international affairs are regularly defined in terms of the military metaphysic. For the professional military, domestic policies are important mainly as ways of retaining and enlarging the military establishment. That is their business; that is what they are trained for. Their careers and their kind of honor are tied up with the war machine. So long as they remain professional soldiers their training and their way of life tend to incapacitate them for transcending the military metaphysic.

v. The ascendancy of military personnel is due less to any greed for power on their part than to the civilian default of political power. Politicians, hiding behind the supposed ex-

pertise of testifying and of advising warlords, have abdicted their proper job of debating and deciding policies. Political administrators have abdicated their proper job of creating and maintaining a really civilian and a really professional senior civil service. It is in the vacuum created by such political abdications and hesitations that the military ascendancy has occurred. It is because of this political vacuum that the warlords have been drawn—often unwillingly—into the higher political decisions. Once there, they are sometimes criticized and even become centers of controversy. Let us remember that they must often operate in an inherited context of civilian distrust and that, being used to command in their rigid bureaucracy, they do not take well to criticism. Some withdraw in a rigid, soldierly way; they stiffen into political aloofness. Those who do not withdraw cannot usually become openly political in the party sense. But they can, and they do, form alliances and pro-military cliques with political figures and with corporation executives. Thus does the military get into politics and politics get into the military —and in both spheres there is the man from the corporation. Such, in brief, is one major focus of elite power in America today—and one leading cause of the drift and the thrust toward World War III.

10—THE PERMANENT

WAR ECONOMY

SINCE the end of World War II many in elite circles have felt that economic prosperity in the U. S. is immediately underpinned by the war economy and that desperate economic—and so political—problems might well arise should there be disarmament and genuine peace. Conciliatory gestures by the Russians are followed by stock-market selling. When there is fear that negotiations may occur, let alone that a treaty structure for the world be arranged, stocks, by their jitters, reflect what is called a "peace scare." When unemployment increases and there is demand that something be done, government spokesmen regularly justify themselves by referring first of all to increases in the money spent and to be spent for war preparations. Thus with unemployment at 4.5 million in January 1958, the President proclaimed that war-contract awards will rise from the $35.6 billion of 1957 to the $47.2 billion of 1958.

These connections between economic conditions and war preparations are not obscure and hidden; they are publicly and regularly reported. And they are definitely among the causes for elite acceptance of the military metaphysic and hence among the causes of World War III.

Back of these well-reported facts are the structural connections between the privately incorporated economy and the military ascendancy. Leading corporations now profit from the preparation of war. Insofar as the business elite are aware of their profit interests—and that is their responsible business—they press for a continuation of their sources of profit, which often means a continuation of the preparation for war. As sources of political advice and as centers of power, higher business and higher military circles share an interest in the felt need for armament and for its continual and wasteful development. We cannot assay with accuracy the causal weight of this personnel and their interests, but the combination of a seemingly "permanent war economy" and a "privately incorporated economy" cannot reasonably be supposed to be an unambiguous condition for the making of peace.

I am *not* suggesting that military power is now only, or even mainly, an instrument of economic policy. To a considerable extent, militarism has become an end in itself and economic policy a means of it. Moreover, whatever the case in previous periods of capitalism, in our immediate times war in each country is being prepared in order to prevent another country from becoming militarily stronger. "There is much justification," E. H. Carr has noted, "for the epi-

gram that 'the principal cause of war is war itself.' " Perhaps
at no previous period has this been so much the case as now,
for the means of war, and war as a means, have never before
been so absolute as to make war so economically irrational.

But we must remember that true capitalist brinkmanship
consists of the continual preparation for war, just short of it;
and that such brinkmanship does have economic functions
of important capitalist consequence. Moreover, it is by no
means clear that the American elite realize the economic ir-
rationality of war itself. In the meantime, an expensive arms
race, under cover of the military metaphysic and in a paranoid
atmosphere of fright, is an economically attractive business.
To many utopian capitalists, it has become The Business
Way of American Life.

I cannot here examine the economics of World War II,
but it is relevant to understand that the corporate elite of
America have ample reason to remember it well. In the four
years following 1940, some $175 billion worth of prime
supply contracts—the keys to control of the nation's means
of production—were given to private corporations. Naturally enough, two thirds went to the top one hundred corporations—in fact, almost one third went to ten private corporations. These companies were granted priorities and allot-
ments for materials and parts; they decided how much of
these were to be passed down to subcontractors. They were
allowed to expand their own facilities under extremely favorable amortization (20 per cent a year) and tax privileges
(instead of the normal twenty or thirty years, they could
write off the cost in five). In general these were the same
corporations that operated most of the government-owned
facilities and obtained favorable options to "buy" them after
the war.

It had cost some $40 billion to build all the manufacturing facilities existing in the United States in 1939. By 1945 an additional $26 billion worth of high-quality new plant and equipment had been added—two thirds of it paid for directly from government funds. Some $20 billion of this $26 billion worth was usable for producing peacetime goods. If to the $40 billion existing we add this $20 billion, we have a $60-billion productive plant usable in the postwar period. In 1939, the top two hundred and fifty corporations owned about 65 per cent of the facilities then existing; during the war, they operated 79 per cent of all new privately operated facilities built with government money; as of September 1944, they held 78 per cent of all active prime-war-supply contracts.

The economic boom of World War II—and only that— pulled the U.S.A. out of the slump of the thirties. After that war a flood of pent-up demand was let loose. To this was added the production of war materials of conventional and unconventional sort. The result, as everyone knows, was the great American prosperity of the last decade.

In the winter of 1957–58 another recession began in the United States. By late March, some six million were unemployed. The mechanics of this recession were generally familiar. There was an "overextension" of capitalist investment in the early fifties, perhaps due to favorable tax amortization; then the rate of capital formation dropped. There was an increase in the installment debt—a mortgaging of future income—especially during 1955. At the same time there has been an arrogant rigidity of prices set by corporate administrators. In fact some prices (for example, steel) were administered up rather than down—even in the face of declining demand—and production was cut.

To this old capitalist folly, Dr. John Blair has recently revealed, there has now been added a rather direct link between "the mode of compensation" for corporation executives and the rigidity or even the increase of the prices they administer. The stock options given these executives connect their income and wealth to dividends or to the market value of common stock, thus avoiding taxes payable on salaries. Price increases, it is well known, tend to raise stock prices. The long-term compensation of the business elite is thus tied to rising prices and to rising stock values, rather than to lower costs and lower prices.*

The recession could of course be fought by vigorous price reductions, even imposed by government price controls; by a cut in taxes to increase purchasing power; and by a very large public-works program, perhaps for school facilities. Such means, which are theoretically at the disposal of the capitalist slump-fighter, are now generally accepted by liberal and by conservative economists. Perhaps such means would be economically adequate. They do not, however, seem to be politically acceptable to everyone involved in the decisions; they do not seem to be altogether acceptable to the capitalists of the Eisenhower Administration.

There is always another way open to them: expenditures for war as a capitalist subsidy and as a countervailing force to capitalist slump. Such expenditures have been most efficiently wasteful, and they often seem to be politically unarguable.

It is not relevant to my argument that this particular recession either deepen or be overcome. My point is that slump—for so long as it is felt as a threat—will further

---

* See "Report of the Subcommittee on Antitrust and Monopoly," S. Res. 1957, 85th Congress, First Session. (U. S. Government Printing Office, 1958.)

harden the militarist posture of the U. S. elite, and that this elite has attempted and will attempt to overcome it by still larger military expenditure. It is of course not that simple, but neither is it so complex as to be incomprehensible. International tensions, incidents, crises do not just happen. The definitions of world reality held by both sides of the encounter, as well as continual default, enter into such international affairs. Slump in America will stiffen these war-making definitions and will serve as additional excuse for the continued lack of decision; it will increase the tension; it will make more likely and more frightening the incidents; it will sharpen the perilous crisis. The fear of slump in America cannot reasonably be considered a context that will increase the American elite's contribution to the making of peace. In their interplay with Soviet decision-makers it is more likely to increase their contribution to the thrust and the drift toward World War III.

Yet it is a hard fact for capitalism that the new weaponry, the new kinds of war preparations, do not seem to be as economically relevant to subsidizing the defaults and irrationalities of the capitalist economy as the old armament and preparations. The amount of money spent is large enough, but it tends to go to a smaller proportion of employees, to the technician rather than to the semiskilled. The people who make missiles and bombs will probably not put into consumption as high a ratio of their incomes as would the more numerous makers of tanks and aircraft. Accordingly, the new type of military pump-priming will not prime as much; it will not carry as great a "multiplier effect"; it will not stimulate consumption or subsidize capitalism as well as the older type. It is a real capitalist difficulty, and the military expenditures may indeed have to be great to overcome it.

Ten years ago, in *The New Men of Power*, I noted that "if the sophisticated conservatives have their way, the next New Deal will be a war economy rather than a welfare economy. . . . In the last transition from peace to war, WPA was replaced by WPB. . . . The establishment of a permanent war economy is a long-time trend. Its pace and tactics will vary according to the phase of the slump-war-boom cycle dominant at any given time. In the phase of inflated boom with great fear of slump, the practical rightists [of the smaller business classes] have the initiative, but in the longer historical perspective, they are merely advance shock troops of the big right. Carrying out the old-fashioned policies of the practical conservatives will lead straight to slump. Then the sophisticated conservatives will take over policy-making for the business class as a whole."

That, I believe, is what we have been witnessing in the Eisenhower Administration.

Many sophisticated conservatives, it would seem, have taken seriously the capitalist image of the world so widely set forth at the end of World War II. "We are asking the U. S. businessman," *Fortune* editorialists then wrote, "to think of Wendell Willkie's 'One World' not in fancy geopolitical terms, but merely in market terms." In describing the glories of capitalist expansion in terms of what father and son did, they ask: "Is this expansion from local iron-monger to 'national distribution' ordained to stop there? The task of expanding trade in stovepipe from a national to an international range is a tricky and often exasperating business, but there is money in it."

There must be: American export of goods and services amounted to $26 billion in 1957; in addition, twenty-five hundred U. S. firms with branches or subsidies abroad sold some $32 billion. The U. S. "foreign market" is $58 billion a year. "Foreign earnings," *Fortune* wrote in January 1958, "will more than double in ten years, more than twice the probable gain in domestic profits." Moreover, "average foreign investment in 1956 and 1957" was probably close to $6 billion. The total invested in 1957 ($37.5 billion) was "roughly double what it was in 1950." Given present rates of increase, it seems likely that, a decade from now, private foreign investment will rise to nearly $60 billion.

Imperialism has generally meant the political and, if need be, the military protection of businessmen and their interests in foreign areas. The political protection need not include the conquest of colonies; the military protection need not involve the establishment of bases and garrisons. But regardless of the manner of the protection extended, imperialism by definition involves the interplay of economic, political, and military institutions and men. No event of significance can be understood without understanding how these interests come to points of clash or of coincidence. "The international system" of the world today cannot be understood without understanding the changing forms of their interplay.

In thinking about "imperialism" we must be prepared to develop different theories for different periods and for different kinds of political economies. The pre-1914 situation, for example, was quite different from the post-1945 scene, in which two superstates of quite distinctive structure confront each other around the world, and in which specific ruling coalitions of economic, political, and military agents are quite unique.

Both Russia and America are "imperialistic" in the service of their ideas and in their fears about military and political security. It is in the economic element that they differ.

The economic aim of Soviet imperialism is simply booty.

Such imperialism consists of the political control of an area with the aim of (1) accumulating valuable capital goods or (2) extracting agricultural and other "surpluses"—as in the Stalinist exploitation of Eastern Europe. Such efforts, as in capitalist imperialism, result in keeping the "colonial" country from industrialization, in keeping it as a producer of raw materials. The economic nature of Soviet imperialism does not arise from any "contradiction" in the Soviet economy; economically, it is simply brutal conquest. But as the Soviet economy is further industrialized, this kind of imperialist temptation and drive loses its strength. The reverse is the case with capitalist imperialism.

The aim of capitalist imperialism is, at first, to open up markets for the export of "surplus" consumer goods, and to use the colonial country as a producer of raw materials which the industrial nation needs in its manufacturing. Manufactured goods, in turn, are sold to the backward country. In due course, however, the backward region becomes a sphere for the investment of capital accumulated by the advanced nation. Such export of capital requires, in the capitalist view, that the risk be limited by political guarantees. Only when the state will assure the capitalist that it will support and protect him can such risky investments be undertaken on any scale. After the investment is made there is naturally an expectation or a demand that it be backed up politically. Only a highly organized capitalist group can expect to exert such influence within and upon the state. For example, the oil corporations.

Oil is a key industry in the making of U. S. foreign policies and of U. S. foreign obstinacies. The elites of this industry are experienced in dealing with governments at home and abroad. They will take risks and ask for help where, for example, steel's elite would hesitate, if only out of inexperience. Oil men do not want war, but their interests are such that they will gamble further than most other industries. They are not "merchants of death"; they are merchants of oil. But they cannot very well be pure-and-simple oil men. They are also political men. They are among the capitalist brinkmen. And in this they have been well represented, particularly in the Middle East, by Secretary of State John Foster Dulles.

Apart from Latin America, which I shall not discuss here, the Middle East is the prime locale of U. S. imperialist gambling, and oil of course is the key industry involved. Seven enormous companies, the Federal Trade Commission's staff reported in 1952, dominate the oil scene of the Middle East. They favor, L. P. Elwell-Sutton—an expert observer—has remarked, "stable, cautious, paternalistic regimes, and frown on governments that show themselves too responsive to fluctuations in public opinion, too ready to indulge in social and economic experiment."

One of the most important documents of the Middle East crisis of 1956 was revealed by Estes Kefauver in the U. S. Senate a week or so before the Eisenhower Doctrine was proclaimed.* On August 13, 1956, "a meeting was held of the Foreign Petroleum Supply Committee, at which were present representatives of the major oil companies and officials of various governmental agencies. . . . Secretary Dulles 'spoke for about fifteen minutes on matters involved in the current Middle East crisis.' Unfortunately the minutes do not give any indication of what Secretary Dulles actually said. However, the representative of one of the major oil companies who had been present wrote a memorandum describing what had transpired at the meeting, a copy of which has

* *Congressional Record*—Senate—March 1, 1957, pp. 2550 ff.

been secured by the committee. . . . In essence, Secretary Dulles was indicating his awareness of the oil companies' concern over the prospect of nationalization of their property; he was acknowledging the general right of sovereign countries to nationalize property; but he was making two qualifications to that right: First, that adequate compensation would have to be paid; and second, that properties 'impressed with international interests' could not be nationalized. The Secretary's conclusion is worth repeating: 'Therefore'—he indicated—'nationalization of this kind of an asset impressed with international interest was far beyond compensation of shareholders alone and should call for international intervenion.'

"Assuming that this is a correct account of what Secretary Dulles said," Senator Kefauver continued, "the Congress of the United States, before it passes the resolution [the Eisenhower Doctrine], has a right to know what Secretary Dulles meant. . . . Who, for example, is going to do the intervening? There is no indication that United States troops would not be used for this purpose, and what, may I ask, would Russia's reaction be to that?

"If the resolution is passed, the Congress would, in effect, be giving up its right to debate the question of whether our national interest does, in fact, warrant intervention by United States troops to prevent the nationalization of concessions held by giant oil companies."

The resolution was duly passed. The crises of the Middle East continued to accumulate. In July 1958, Senator Kefauver's questions were answered and the meaning of the Eisenhower Doctrine made plain: U. S. Marines were landed in Lebanon. British paratroopers were sent to Jordan. The U. S. and the British governments announced that they would not invade Iraq unless the government of that country failed, as *The New York Times* reported, to "respect Western oil interests." Thus did the power elite attempt, in official language, "to assure the independence and integrity of these two small countries," or, in the unofficial terms of the *Times* reporter, Dana Adams Schmidt: "to restore Western prestige generally in the Middle East and to stabilize the friendly oil-producing governments in Saudi Arabia and the Persian Gulf region."

11—THE WORLD ENCOUNTER

WE ARE still witnessing what surely must be called "imperialism," but we have also gone beyond it. The economic interests and fears of the American and the Russian power elite must now be seen in still a larger context.

For the first time in human history an advanced capitalist economy is in world encounter with an alternative way of industrialization. That is the world historical meaning of the Russian Revolution. By its industrial success, the Soviet system has proved that there is a way to industrialize backward countries without resort to the older capitalist way of the West. Moreover, the appeal of Soviet communism to strategic agents of change in underdeveloped countries is attested to by the historical fact that, with one or possibly two exceptions, only in such countries has communism been successfully installed as a political and economic way of life.

In the preindustrial countries, Russian propaganda has many assets: Most of these countries contain colored races—and Russia is free of color prejudice. They are illiterate and impoverished—as was Russia only two generations ago. They inherit much ill will toward capitalist behavior of a colonial sort; they have become aware that Western capitalism has failed over a three-hundred-year period to put through industrialization in these areas. Moreover, the underdeveloped countries are in a hurry and the Soviet way is fast. To these peoples it often seems at once utopian and practical. The intellectuals of the underdeveloped world, as well as the people generally, know how far from reality capitalist notions of industrialization now seem for them; more decisively, they are coming to believe that their countries will remain underdeveloped so long as they accept such notions. Accordingly many of these people, quite understandably, look to Russia as a model of their own future.

The industrialization of the world is the master trend of our time; perhaps it is not inevitable, but it is strong enough as a demand and appealing enough as a promise to set the key terms of the world-wide competition between the two dominant systems of economic, military and political power. That the underdeveloped countries—containing two thirds of mankind—are still underdeveloped is a world historical default of Western capitalism. Colonialism and the attempted "Balkanization" of China in the nineteenth century and of the Middle East after 1918, the active support of feudal classes—and worse, of slavery and nationalistic backwardness in all its meanings—all this has been a long and tortuous default. But never has this been so explicit as now; never has it been the basis of a world crisis. Only in this context can the Russian successes in underdeveloped countries be understood. The West has failed to show non-Western peoples a sensible way to become industrial and has failed to help them to do so. One has only to look briefly at recent Chinese events to realize how plainly this is the case.

The coexistence of China and India—together they contain one third of all the people in the world—is now a pivot of world history. Both have thrown off white rule. Both have not only "manpower" but resources. Yet the name of India is a synonym for poverty. In Calcutta and in other Indian cities some 10 per cent of the population exist day and night on the streets. India is fumbling for a plan, and she is not doing very well. But China, under Communist rule, is clearly advancing in an industrial way. What the Russians have done industrially in forty years, China may well do in twenty-five.

Backward economies *can* be "modernized" more or less on their own, but this seems to require dictatorial regimes which will sweat out of a generation or two the primary accumulation of capital goods needed. Backward economies can also be modernized, perhaps more slowly, without dictatorial regimes, but this seems to require that they be greatly and intelligently helped by industrially advanced nations. There do not seem to be other alternatives.

China—that is to say, 650,000,000 of the world's population—does not exist in the official view of the U.S.A. India—where the crisis of democracy in Asia is fully revealed—is receiving so little U. S. help as to be a world joke on capitalism's ability to help industrialize primitive economies. In the meantime two thirds of mankind wait and watch.

In Asia, communism is older than any democratic left, and if the two together are considered the "left," there is no

question—as Saul Rose, a British commentator, has recently
indicated—that the left is predominant in Asia. In the non-
Communist lands from Pakistan to Japan, people generally
live under governments professing socialism. This leftward
trend rests upon nationalism. There are of course exceptions,
due, as in small countries like Nepal and Laos, to uncertain
political conditions; as in South Korea and South Vietnam,
to civil war and stalemate with Communists; or, as in Japan
and Thailand, to the fact that nationalist movements have not
been needed to throw off foreign rule, for they were never
colonialized. But this belt of countries is more or less a natural
fringe of China and of India; the first is flourishing as Communist, the second is struggling as proclaimed Socialist but
with rising Communist influence.

The American elite is becoming aware that the political
economy of communism may very well outcompete, in their
own terms of production, the political economy of capitalism.
That point has now been made dramatic by the high-flying
products of the Russian Science Machine. The collective economy of Russia and its great potential for production and
productivity, for innovation, for distribution, are seen correctly as an economic and a political threat to the capitalist
political economy of the U.S.A.

Conservative estimates by American experts are that the
Russian economy has been growing by at least 6 per cent a
year; the long-term American average is about 3 per cent.
If we assume no slump in the U. S., the Soviets will overtake
the U. S. economy in a mere decade, or at most two. The
Soviet economy is subject to many strains, but it is not subject to capitalist slump. Moreover its economic growth is not
going into two television sets in every home but into machine tools for China, not into stupidly designed and stupidly

engineered automobiles but into capital equipment—as well as rockets. The use of Soviet economic growth is relevant not only to weaponry but to basic economic development.

The same skills and resources that launched a ton-and-a-half moon in all probability can result in an automated flood of consumer goods; there are no internal technical, political, or economic reasons why these skills and resources should not be so used in the near future. The Russian boast of coming production is not bluff. Soon Russia is going to be, in the same sense that America now is, a first-rate industrial power.

The Soviet way of forced, speedy industrialization has been and is a brutal way. It has not led to such freedoms as the West has known; this brutality and tyranny cannot be justified by pointing out the brutality and tyranny of earlier capitalist exploitation (such as that of children in British mines a century ago). Nor is the insensibility of Soviet decision-makers excused by that of the American decision-makers who caused the first A-bombs to be dropped—without warning, without demonstration, without ultimatum—on civilian populations. Both are brutal; both display the inhuman lack of sensibility characteristic of underdeveloped men in overdeveloped societies, of men with rationality but without reason.

But the U. S. elite are doctrinaire capitalists, which means —given present world economic conditions—that they are utopian capitalists as well. I do not believe that they know of any way, in which even *they* really believe, to maintain their capitalist interests and at the same time to industrialize the underdeveloped world. In the economic and political world of today, I do not think that U. S. capitalism is an exportable system. The U. S. elite are now losing the contest to determine the pattern of world industrialization. They have not got the diplomatic or the technical skills required. And they have not got the will to do it. They "give foreign aid" for military reasons, and they invest for reasons of profit; but when there is neither capitalist profit nor military relevance, then little or nothing is available.

There is no comprehensive plan, no systematic idea, no general program for the economic development of India, Latin America, the Middle East, Africa, Southeast Asia. There are only spotty and episodic grants and loans, covered up by the slogans of realism and practicality, by doctrinaire capitalism and the military metaphysic.

Considering the world economic situation of utopian capitalism, one is reminded of Karl Marx's remark of 1853: "Impotence expresses itself in a single proposition: the maintenance of the status quo." That status quo now includes the thrust toward World War III. By definition, the insane are unpredictable, but often they are also consistently obstinate, perhaps especially when they become vaguely aware that they may well be headed toward bankruptcy. By the obstinacy of their default they reveal, as Marx said, "their complete incapacity to further the cause of progress and civilization."

That communism may not serve this cause any better than capitalism is not the major point. The point is that Russia may well win the world struggle without firing a single missile and that the Soviet elite may well be willing to conduct the struggle in economic terms. The seeming inability or unwillingness of the U. S. elite to do so is a major cause of World War III.

12—ON PSYCHOLOGICAL
CAUSES

THE STRATEGIC causes of World War III, I have been arguing, are direct and immediate. Only if we assume a direct and immediate democracy of power can we assume that "the people" have an immediate and active part in such history-making decisions as are involved in this thrust. Neither for the Soviet Union nor for the United States can we make such an assumption; the part of people in general in the thrust is at most permissive or hampering. In the U.S.A., in fact, publics are becoming politically indifferent; they are being rapidly transformed into masses; and these masses are becoming morally as well as politically insensible.

Yet many commentators hold the view that the opinions of innumerable people, or even generic "human nature," are among the causes of war. More recently, psychologists and anthropologists have ascribed war to "misunderstandings" between "peoples" or, more sophisticatedly, to "the tensions arising from differences in national character." This is a very old view, although it now masquerades in the garb of social science.

Rousseau and Kant argued that since wars were waged by princes in their own interests and not in that of their peoples, there would be no wars under a republican form of government. More recently, many men of good will have publicized the view that war is due to a "failure of understanding," that peace is a matter of rationally convincing enough of the public that war is absurd.

To hold such a view, I believe, requires us to assume that people in general are directly responsible for history-making, and so for war-making; it is to assume that a direct and total democracy of power prevails, rather than a condition in which history-making power is decisively centralized. Such notions, once they are fully elaborated, turn out, I believe, to be variations of the idea of fate which I have already explained in a sociological way. Often enough, too, those who hold such views come to talk of tragic guilt, usually that of "other people," rather than of political responsibility. Such programs for peace often come down, contradictorily, to educational programs—usually directed toward the people of nations whose elites have behaved badly and stupidly.

The vague notion that war is due to tense differences of "national character," along with the assumption that power rests with the people, seems to me more than mistaken and less than useful. It is part of the nationalist trap. Increased "understanding" may just as well lead to more intelligent hatred as to greater love. To have understood better the Nazi character and outlook would not necessarily have led to avoidance of war with Nazis.

Better understanding between peoples does not necessarily result in, much less determine, changes in the policies of their respective elites. To believe that it does is to assume that the policies of all governments are a simple mirror of the opinions of national populations; or it is to endow, as Dwight MacDonald once put it, a nation or a people with "qualities of will and choice that belong in reality only to individuals. . . . This animistic confusion marks the common man's thinking (with plenty of help from his political rulers) not only on relations between nations but also on the relation of the state and the individual citizen. Precisely because in this sphere the individual is most powerless in reality, do his rulers make their greatest efforts to present the state not only as an instrument for *his* purposes but as an extension of *his* personality. They have to try to do this because of the emphasis on the free individual which the bourgeois revolution has made part of our political assumptions. . . . The theory is convenient for those in power on two scores: Internally, it preserves the ladder of hierarchy, making rebellious behavior treason not only to those in authority but also to the alleged common interests of everybody, to what is reverently termed 'national unity' these days; in time of war, it makes it possible to treat the enemy population as a homogeneous single block, all of them equally wicked and detestable."

The issues of war and peace cannot be melted down into a naïve psychology of "peace through better understanding among peoples." It is not the aggression of people in general but their mass indifference that is the point of their true political and psychological relevance to the thrust toward war.

It is neither the "psychology of peoples" nor raw "human nature" that is relevant; it is the moral insensibility of people who are selected, molded, and honored in the mass society.

In this new society there has come about a situation in which many who have lost faith in prevailing loyalties have not acquired new ones, and so they pay no attention to politics of any kind. They are not radical, not liberal, not conservative, not reactionary. They are inactionary. They are out of it. If we accept the Greek definition of the idiot as an altogether private man, then we must conclude that many American and many Soviet citizens are now idiots. This spiritual condition—and I choose the phrase with care—is the key to many contemporary problems as well as to much political bewilderment. Intellectual "conviction" and moral "belief" are not necessary, in either the ruled or the rulers, for a ruling power to persist and even to flourish. The prevalence of mass indifference is surely one of the major political facts about the Western societies today.

As it concerns the thrust toward war this indifference is best seen as moral insensibility: the mute acceptance—or even unawareness—of moral atrocity; the lack of indignation when confronted with moral horror; the turning of this atrocity and this horror into morally approved conventions of feeling. By moral insensibility, in short, I mean the incapacity for *moral* reaction to event and to character, to high decision and to the drift of human circumstance.

Such insensibility has its roots in World War I; it became full-blown during World War II. The "saturation bombing" of that war was often the indiscriminate bombing of civilian populations on a mass scale, as was the atomic bombing of the peoples of Hiroshima and Nagasaki. That Hiroshima was more sudden and more impersonal than Auschwitz, whatever other moral differences may be discerned, makes it none the less immoral. One should reflect carefully on how far they must be bracketed together in the record of moral insensibility and the deformation of humanity. By the time of Korea, at any rate, the principle of obliteration had become totally accepted as part of the moral universe of the mass society.

In this society, between catastrophic event and everyday interests there is a vast moral gulf. How many in North America experienced, as human beings, World War II? Few rebelled, few knew public grief. It was a curiously unreal business, full of efficiency without purpose. A sort of numbness seemed to prohibit any awareness of what was happening; it was without dream and so without nightmare, and if there were anger and fear and hatred—and there were—still no torrent of feeling and conviction and compassion was let loose in despair or furor; little human complaint was focused rebelliously upon the political and moral meaning of the universal brutality. Masses sat in the movies between production shifts watching with aloofness and even visible indifference as children were "saturation bombed" in the narrow cellars of European cities. Man had become an object; and insofar as those to whom he was an object felt about the spectacle at all, they felt powerless, in the grip of larger forces, with no part in those affairs that lay beyond their immediate areas of daily demand and gratification. It was a time of moral somnambulance.

In the expanded world of mechanically vivified communication the individual becomes the spectator of everything but the human witness of nothing. Having no plain targets of revolt, men feel no moral springs of revolt. The cold manner enters their souls and they are made private and blasé. In virtually all realms of life, facts now outrun sensibility. Emptied of their human meanings, these facts are readily got used to. In official man there is no more human shock; in his unofficial follower there is little sense of moral issue. Within the unopposed supremacy of impersonal, calculated technique, there is no human place to draw the line and give the emphatic no.

This lack of response I am trying to sum up by the phrase "moral insensibility," and I am suggesting that the level of moral sensibility, as part of public and of private life, has sunk out of sight. It is not the number of victims or the degree of cruelty that is distinctive; it is the fact that the acts committed and the acts that nobody protests are split from the consciousness of men in an uncanny, even a schizophrenic, manner. The atrocities of our time are done by men as "functions" of a social machinery—men possessed by an abstracted view that hides from them the human beings who are their victims and, as well, their own humanity. They are inhuman acts because they are impersonal. They are not sadistic but merely businesslike; they are not aggressive but merely efficient; they are not emotional at all but technically clean-cut.

This insensibility was made dramatic by the Nazis; but the same lack of human morality prevailed among fighter pilots in Korea, with their petroleum-jelly broiling of children and women and men. And is not this lack raised to a higher and technically more adequate level among the brisk generals and gentle scientists who are now planning the weapons and the strategy of World War III?

We must, I think, assume that in the event of this war, statesmen will order the use of every weapon they think useful to "destroy the enemy," and that masses of men will accept it. For today if men are acting in the name of "their nation," they do not know moral limits but only expedient calculations. Is not that obvious from the history of the last twenty years? Is not that the meaning of the word "barbarism" as applied to our times, and of the single most absolute and fetishized of our values: that of The Nation itself? Among the higher circles of all leading nations, the force of moral restraint is merely one factor, rather a negligible one, to be considered among expedient calculations of "morale," psychological warfare, and what is curiously still called "public opinion."

13—CRACKPOT REALISM

IT IS time to sum up and to make a new beginning. War is now a structural feature of the leading societies of the world; it is also the major activity of identifiable men, performed in the name of the leading states of the world and with their means of national power. World War III, I have been arguing, is being prepared and coldly fought in the name of the sovereign state by the power elites of the two superpowers, with the acquiescence of public and masses and the defaults of political men and intellectual workmen.

The history of our time is not a matter of fate. Decisions —and ideas—do count in what is going to happen. Insofar as this is so, I think we may now, in summary, assert the following:

I. The immediate cause of World War III is the military preparation of it. The nature of the arms race is such that it is not and cannot reasonably be considered a cause of peace. Given the new weaponry and the strategic impasse, it cannot be considered a means of any nation's defense, for the distinction between attack and defense is now meaningless.

II. The immediate causes of the arms race are the official definitions of world reality clung to by the elites of the U.S.A. and of the U.S.S.R. These nationalist definitions and ideologies now serve as the mask behind which elite irresponsibility and incompetence are hidden; they are traps for any attempt to reason seriously and adequately about war as a political issue, and about peace as the moral keystone of a human program.

III. The official theory of war—the military metaphysic— is itself among the causes of the thrust toward war. The less adequate one's definitions of reality and the less apt one's program for changing it, the more complex does the scene of action appear. "Complexity" is not inherent in any phenomena; it is relative to the conceptions with which we approach reality. It is the task of those who want peace to identify causes and to clarify them to the point of action. It is the inadequate definition of world reality and the lack of any imaginative program for peace that make the international scene appear now so complex and hopeless to the American elite, that make perilous those piecemeal reactions which constitute much of U. S. official action and lack of action since the decision to obliterate Hiroshima.

IV. It is in the continual preparation for war that the power elite now finds the major basis for the furthering of the several and the coinciding interests of its members. The military metaphysic justifies their fumbling control and their competition over the enlarged and centralized means of violence, production, and administration. For the professional warlords, this metaphysic is a natural assumption. It is in line with their training and in line with their professional interests and their personal careers.

v. For the politicians, the military metaphysic provides a cover under which they can abdicate the perils of innovative leadership; it provides a cover for their use of military bureaucrats—the only large pool of professional civil servants available—instead of building a civilian civil service of real integrity; it hides the political vacuum in which they now irresponsibly commit their political defaults.

vi. For the corporation executives, the military metaphysic often coincides with their interest in a stable and planned flow of profit; it enables them to have their risks underwritten by public money; it enables them reasonably to expect that they can exploit for private profit, now and later, the risky research developments paid for by public money. It is, in brief, a mask of the subsidized capitalism from which they extract profit and upon which their power is based.

vii. In the West, especially in the United States, there is fear of economic slump should the preparations for war cease or even be slackened off. Corporate interests are being served by the continual design and production of weapons which are obsolete before their completion. Behind these economic motives and interests there is the world confrontation of the capitalist economy and the collectivist economy of the Communist bloc. Increasingly these two political economies compete as models for the industrialization of a world that is largely preindustrial. The U. S. capitalist elite is losing this competition; with good reason, it fears that it will continue to lose.

VIII. The monolithic assumptions of the military metaphysic and the thrust toward war which follows from it are due not alone to the military ascendancy or to the private incorporation of the economy and its capitalist mechanics. These, I believe, *are* causes; but they are able to operate as causes largely because of civilian hesitations and political vacillation. Military and corporate elites have been able to come together and share higher decisions, as well as to make them separately, because of the fact of the political vacuum.

In the U.S.A. today, there are no nationally responsible political parties offering and standing upon alternative political orientations and programs. There is no significant senior civil service composed of professional men whose careers are secure and independent of private interests. The leading men of the U. S. government—the political directorate—are neither professional party politicians nor professional civil servants; they are former generals and former corporation men or the hangers-on of the higher business and legal circles. The state in which we live, in its personnel and in its persistent outlook, does indeed appear at times as a committee of these ruling circles of corporation and high military.

IX. Economic and military causes of war are allowed to operate also because of the political apathy of publics and the moral insensibility of masses in both Communist and capitalist worlds, and by the political inactivity and abdication of leading intellectual circles of these worlds. The roles of publics and of masses in U. S. developments are generally negligible and permissive, although often uneasily so. But publics and masses are held by the feeling that they and their elites as well are in the grip of fate. They do not know how to raise demands with effect; they are powerless and they are morally insensible.

x. The same kind of role is being played by leading intellectual, scientific, and religious circles. Most cultural workmen are fighting a cold war in which they echo and elaborate the confusions of officialdoms. They neither raise demands on the elites for alternative policies, nor set forth such alternatives before publics and masses. Many intellectuals do nothing to fill the political vacuum; indeed, as they fight the cold war, they proclaim, justify, and practice the moral insensibility that is one of its accompaniments. Technologists and scientists readily develop new weapons; preachers and rabbis and priests bless the great endeavor; newsmen disseminate the official definitions of world reality, labeling for their publics the shifting line-up of friends and enemies; publicists elaborate the "reasons" for the coming war, and the "necessity" for the causes of it. They do not set forth alternative policies; they do not politically oppose and politically debate the thrust toward war. They have generally become the Swiss Guard of the power elite—Russian or American, as the case happens to be. Unofficial spokesmen of the military metaphysic, they have not lifted the level of moral sensibility; they have further depressed it. They have not tried to put responsible content into the political vacuum; they have helped to empty it and to keep it empty. What must be called the Christian default of the clergy is part of this sorry moral condition and so is the capture of scientists by nationalist Science Machines. The journalistic lie, become a routine, is part of it too, and so is the pretentious triviality of much that passes for social science.

XI. The thrust toward World War III is *not* a plot on the part of the elite, either that of the U.S.A. or that of the U.S.S.R. Among both, there are "war parties" and "peace parties," and among both there are what can be called crackpot realists. These are men who are so rigidly focused on the next step that they become creatures of whatever the main drift—the opportunist actions of innumerable men—brings. They are also men who cling rigidly to general principles. The frenzied next step plus the altogether general principle equal U. S. foreign policy—of which Mr. Dulles has been so fine an exemplar. In crackpot realism, a high-flying moral rhetoric is joined with an opportunist crawling among a great scatter of unfocused fears and demands. In fact, the main content of "politics" is now a struggle among men equally expert in practical next steps—which, in summary, make up the thrust toward war—and in great, round, hortatory principles. But without any program.

XII. Programs require that next steps be reasonably linked with principled images of a goal. To act toward goals requires that the next step be consciously worked out in terms of its consequences, and that these consequences be weighed and valued in terms of the goal. Lacking a program, the opportunist moves short distances among immediate and shifting goals. He reacts rather than inaugurates, and the directions of his reactions are set less by any goals of his own than by the circumstances to which he feels forced to react out of fear and uneasiness. Since he is largely a creature of these circumstances, rather than a master of independent action, the results of his expedient maneuvers and of his defaults are more products of the main drift than of his own vision and will. To be merely expedient is to be in the grip of historical fate or in the grip of those who are not merely expedient.

Sunk in the details of immediate and seemingly inevitable decisions to which he feels compelled to react, the crackpot realist does not know what he will do next; he is waiting for another to make a move.

XIII. The expectation of war solves many problems of the crackpot realists; it also confronts them with many new problems. Yet these, the problems of war, often seem easier to handle. They are out in the open: to produce more, to plan how to kill more of the enemy, to move materials thousands of miles. The terms of the arms race, once the race is accepted as necessary, seem clear; the explicit problems it poses often seem "beyond politics," in the area of administration and technology. War and the planning of war tend to turn anxiety into worry; perhaps, as many seem to feel, genuine peace would turn worry into anxiety. War-making seems a hard technological and administrative matter; peace is a controversial and ambiguous political word. So instead of the unknown fear, the anxiety without end, some men of the higher circles prefer the simplification of known catastrophe.

The official expectation of war also enables men to solve the problems of the economic cycles without resort to political policies that are distasteful to many politicians and to large segments of the American public. The terms of their long-term solution, under conditions of peace, are hard for the capitalist elite to face.

Some of them, accordingly, have come to believe that the world encounter has reached a point where there is no other solution but war, even when they sense that war can be a solution to nothing. They have come to believe this because those in control in each of the countries concerned are trapped by the consequences of their past actions and their present hostile outlook. They live in a world filled with events that overwhelm them. They know of no solutions to the paradoxes of the Middle East and Europe, the Far East and Africa except the landing of Marines. Being baffled, and also being very tired of being baffled, they have come to believe that there is no way out—except war—which would remove all the bewildering paradoxes of their tedious and now misguided attempts to construct peace. In place of these paradoxes they prefer the bright, clear problems of war—as they used to be. For they still believe that "winning" means something, although they never tell us what.

It is because of such bewilderment and frustration, based on the position and the interests of the power elite, that I assume that there have been and are in the U.S.A. and in the U.S.S.R. "war parties," men who want war; and also "peace parties," men who do not want war. Some men want war for sordid, others for idealistic, reasons; some for personal gain, others for impersonal principle. But most of those who consciously want war and accept it, and so help to create its "inevitability," want it in order to shift the locus of their problems.

Moreover, there is a point about war parties that does not hold so firmly for peace parties. The success of the war party in one nation interacts with the success of the war party in the other. When such cliques win in Russia, their counterparts are strengthened in the United States, and vice versa. Thus, when in some debate among decision-makers a war party wins out, it is able to consolidate its gains because its victories accumulate, as does the mutual fright it feeds upon and increases.

xiv. For those who would quietly attain modest goals in a short while, and who are acting within a main drift that is generally beneficent, crackpot realism is quite fitting. They need neither enduring means nor orienting programs of scope. But for those who are in the main drift toward World War III and who would stop that drift and attain a world condition of peace, opportunism is merely a series of cumulative defaults. Short-run pursuits are leading to long-run consequences that are not under the control of any program. The absence of an American program for peace is a major cause of the thrust and drift toward World War III.

In the meantime, and in the absence of such a program, elites of political, military, and economic power are at the focal points of the economic, political, and military causes of war. By their decisions and their indecisions, by their defaults and their ignorance, they control the thrust of these causes. They are allowed to occupy such positions, and to use them in accordance with crackpot realism, because of the powerlessness, the apathy, the insensibility of publics and masses; they are able to do so, in part, because of the inactionary posture of intellectuals, scientists, and other cultural workmen. In both the U. S. and the U.S.S.R., and in the frightened zones that lie between them, there is a political vacuum and an intellectual vacuum. In both, the thrust toward World War III is accelerated by elite behavior in the name of the sovereign state and in accordance with the military metaphysic.

PART THREE—WHAT, THEN, OUGHT WE TO DO?

14—ON THE LOSS OF VISION

To ASK and to answer the question "What is to be done?" is not enough. We must also specify who is to do it. Nowadays, many people have stopped making up programs because they are discouraged about the lack of any leaders who are open to new ideas—or to any ideas at all—and at the same time in a position to use them in history-making decisions. Many people no longer ask the intellectual and moral question "What is to be done?" because their imaginations are paralyzed by the political question of who might do it. As a result, they have abandoned all interest in programs or they have narrowed their imaginations to the limits and interests of a power elite that displays its ignorance in so perilous a manner. Everything not within these limits is considered utopian, naïve, impractical, unrealistic.

The reason, in short, why so many have abandoned the

making of programs is that they see in the United States no real public for such programs. Such a public, in greater or lesser degree, would have to be part of an organization, a movement, a party with a chance to influence the decisions now being made and the defaults now being committed. It would also have to contain people who are at least attentive to ideas and ideals; people among whom one has a chance to get a hearing. When these two conditions are available, one can be programmatic in a "politically realistic" way. When these conditions are not available, then one has this choice:

To modify the ideas, or at least to file them away, and then, temporarily at least, to take up new allegiances and expediencies for which one might work in a "realistic" way. This is the way that is called "practical politics."

The alternative is to retain the ideals, and hence by definition to hold them in a utopian way, while waiting. This is the way that is called impractical and unrealistic.

Of course these two can be combined in various sorts of holding actions, the most usual being the combination of frenzied and "realistic" next steps with great proclamations of principle. Nevertheless there is a real choice between them. As intellectuals and as political men we ought to choose, without qualification, the second way.

We must reject the first way, which perhaps used to be realistic; first, because it has now become merely an abdication of any possible role of reason, indeed of sanity, in human affairs; second, because it amounts to the surrender of any power we might possibly have to those now in charge of the decisions that make history and the decisions not made which might well turn history in other directions; and third, because the near-universal adoption of this "realistic" view by intellectuals is now among the causes of World War III.

We must accept what perhaps used to be the utopian way;

first, because it is now the only adequate way to think about world politics and the human condition; and second, because it is now the only realistic way to work seriously as intellectuals for the conditions of peace. For it must be recognized: What the powerful call utopia is now in fact the condition for human survival.

"A principle, if it be sound," wrote John Morley, "represents one of the larger expediencies. To abandon that for the sake of some seeming expediency of the hour is to sacrifice the greater good for the less, on no more creditable ground than that the less is nearer. It is better to wait and to defer the realization of our ideas until we can realize them fully, than to defraud the future by truncating them, if truncate them we must, in order to secure a partial triumph for them in the immediate present. It is better to bear the burden of impracticableness, than to stifle conviction and pare away principle until it becomes hollowness and triviality."

When we are asked, "What is to be done?" we may answer by raising demands for next steps, by exhortations of general principles, or by statements of a program. Those who have no program say that politics is the art of the possible—and thus beg the key question of politics today. That question is: What is now possible? So far as means are concerned the answer is: It depends upon what position you occupy in the structure of power. So far as ends are concerned the answer is: No one knows the limits of possible human development. What men might become, what kinds of societies men might build—the answers to such questions are neither closed nor inevitable. Yet the discussion of politics has become so dogmatically confined to means, to problems of power, that the ends of which men might dream are consigned to "merely utopian fantasy." In the meantime, virtually all images of the future—from Aldous Huxley's to George Orwell's—have become images of sociological horror, and "practical action" has been usurped by frightened and unimaginative mediocrities.

There are reasons for this condition, but there is no need for it. The root error of judgment involved is the insistence that any vision, demand, hope must be such as to be immediately realizable this week, or at furthest by the next election. If this insistence is dogmatic, as it usually is nowadays, then all political thinking is simply stopped. It is replaced by mere calculations of clique and party strategy; and political responsibility is a mere slogan.

What "practical men of affairs" do not face up to is the fact that "politics" today has to do with the willful making of history. The enlargement and the centralization of the means of history-making signify that, for better or for worse, power elites are no longer in a situation in which their will and reason need be overwhelmed by "impersonal forces beyond their control." A politics of responsibility is now much more possible than in a society with less far-reaching and less centralized means of power. The present fact is otherwise: A politics of semiorganized irresponsibility prevails. But that fact ought not to blind us to the political possibilities opened up by this great structural change: It is now sociologically realistic, morally fair, and politically imperative to make demands upon men of power and to hold them responsible for specific courses of events.

In the meantime, let us for a little while forget the means—we shall return to them—and consider what now ought to be done. I do not suppose the proposals I am going to make to be original; in fact, I take them as obvious reflections of any mind not captured by the official definitions of world reality. At any rate, here are a few guidelines to peace.

15—GUIDELINES, I

WHAT the United States ought to do is abandon the military metaphysic and the doctrinaire idea of capitalism and, in the reasonableness thus gained, reconsider the terms of the world encounter.

I.

WE MUST subvert the monolithic American dogma that now constitutes the one line of elite assumption; we must not allow the elite to identify the foolish choices their view dictates with "military necessity," or to explain its disastrous results by reference to "the evil character of the enemy." Military necessity, we must make clear, has become a cover term by which those who proclaim and who decide in the name of the nation hide their incompetence and their irresponsibility. *The only realistic military view is the view that war, and not Russia, is now the enemy.*

II.

IN THE world disorder of the mid-twentieth century, two thirds of mankind exist in poverty, without adequate means of production. Behind the military struggle is the struggle of the underdeveloped world to become industrial. This struggle, we have seen, the U.S.A. is losing by default and by indifference. In place of the military metaphysic, we must set forth commanding views of the future in which the problems of industrialization are seen as at once the paramount problems of the world today, and the most promising and fruitful issue between the U.S.A. and the U.S.S.R.

We must stress industrialization not as another metaphysic, not as a fetish, not as the solution to all human problems, but as a means of gaining for mankind a suitable standard of living, as a responsibly controlled feature of a properly developing society.

III.

FROM THE standpoint of mere survival, let alone progress toward a world of properly developing societies, there is now one and only one paramount goal and only one general means to it: coexistence.

The United States elite must give up the illusion that "this bunch of Reds" will somehow go away, that their societies

will collapse, or that there is any action short of mutual annihilation that the United States can take to make them collapse. They must recognize the world historical meaning of
the Russian Revolution: that there now exists in the world an
alternative way of industrialization. Abandoning their doctrinaire capitalism, they must recognize that this way works
and that it has great appeal to people of undeveloped areas
who have remained undeveloped for generations in the
epoch of capitalist ascendancy.

We must demand that the coexistence of these two world-
established models of industrialization be fully recognized and
that the competition between them be conducted in economic and cultural and political ways, rather than by means
of the idiot's race.

The military metaphysic must be abandoned.

Industrialization must be seen as the key to the world
struggle.

The world encounter of coexisting political economies
must be conducted in cultural, political, and economic terms.

So crucial are these first three points that if they are taken
literally and seriously they automatically lead to a host of immediate demands and unilateral policies, points to negotiate
and suggestions for co-operative action. So basic are they
that if they were made the guidelines of U. S. policy, within
months the construction of world peace could be well under
way.

IV.

IF PEACE is, and can be only, a peace of coexistence, the means
to peace is, and can be only, negotiation. The structure of

peace has to do with the terms of national competition; the strategy of peace requires the substitution of economic and cultural terms for the military terms that now prevail.

U. S. policy-makers should not automatically reject as propaganda all overtures by the Soviet rulers for global negotiations. Of course, their overtures do also serve as propaganda, but to reject them for that reason is to reveal our policy-makers' own fear—all too often well founded—that they have nothing convincing to say to the world; and it is to display their contempt for the intelligence of the world's peoples.

In the attempt at a new beginning, you do not forget the past; but neither do you allow it to govern the present. What matters today is how a world of properly developing societies can be built out of the impoverished *and* out of the overdeveloped monstrosities that now pass for human societies. And the first and continuing means to that end is negotiation. The encounter is global; the power involved is world-wide and soon perhaps will be universal. The negotiations must now be between those who hold this power and must concern global matters. A reform here, an attempt there, a little bit at a time—that might do, if the over-all structure and its drift were favorable. But when the over-all tendency is, as now, the whole structure, the entire basis of policy must be confronted.

Mr. Dulles repeatedly asserts that he cannot negotiate disarmament with all the members of the United Nations; he is certainly reluctant to do so with only one. Here are two good reasons for replacing him with someone who is not so statistically inhibited. The point is not the composition or size of any one negotiating group. You make a beginning with the powers that be; you try to modify the power and its distribution by expanding the negotiating group.

Negotiation means neither one big conference nor an interminable series of little ones. It means to reason together—continuously, on every level—rather than to carry on exchanges of rhetoric, rather than to negotiate about negotiation. It means to drop the hysterical fears and hatreds brought about by dogmas and petrified attitudes rooted in the status quo. It means to recognize that to assume dogmatically that one can negotiate only from "positions of strength" is merely to declare for the arms race; it means to understand that the "stronger" side at any given time may well be *less* fearful and so more open to reason than the weaker. Negotiation means by continuous effort, on high and on low levels, to relax the tensions and to outline a treaty structure around the globe.

"What faith," it is often asked, "may be placed in any agreement with Moscow?" Put in this way, the question is rather naïve. All nations, as E. H. Carr has demonstrated in detail, tend to keep those agreements which their leaders believe it to be advantageous to keep; they tend to break those which their leaders believe put them at a disadvantage. If one nation breaks more agreements than another, is it not conceivably because, in the past as a weaker nation, she was forced to enter into disadvantageous agreements? That is as true for one nation as for another. The pertinent question now is: Do the Russian elite recognize that World War III would *not* be to Russia's advantage and that an equitable treaty structure presents the only hope for avoiding war? The answer is yes every bit as much for the Russian elite as it is for the American elite.

The Soviet intervention in Hungary might be supposed a ground for believing that agreements with the Soviet would be useless. There is of course no moral excuse for the Russian intervention, but there is a political explanation: given the armaments race, Harry Lustig has suggested, "the Russians felt that they could not afford to let Hungary become at best neutral and at worst another base for American bombers and missiles. . . . It is difficult to compare one evil with another, but at least in the number of people killed the suppression by the French of the Algerian revolution has been every bit as brutal. But no one suggests that it is useless and dangerous to make agreements with France."

V.

SOME 20 per cent of the current U. S. military budget—operational and scientific—should be allocated to the economic aid and industrial development of underdeveloped countries, especially to India. In the next budget, and in each year's thereafter, this amount should be increased by an additional 10 per cent of the total. Tax levels should be kept roughly the same as at present, so that the increasing economic and technical aid can come out of the military budget. Part of the money for industrial development should be used to mount a crash program—if we must use such language for emphasis—for the development of a variety of compact and readily transportable atomic-power plants designed to make electrical power available to all the peoples of the world. At the same time, the beneficiaries must be helped to develop a pattern of skills making possible the proper use of such power. The U. S. should propose that this program be carried out under the authority of the United Nations, and that it should be set up in such ways as to encourage and to enable the people who receive it to participate fully in its planning and its administration.

VI.

IN EVERY culturally underdeveloped area, in the United States as well as elsewhere, the U. S. government, under United Nations auspices, should help to build a first-class educational system and within it set up a program, on a world-wide basis, of circulating professors, teachers, and students. Particular attention should be paid to the humanities and social studies. For as natural science was the issue and the solvent at the ending of the medieval age, just now—within the Soviet bloc especially—it is the social studies and the humanities which could readily become the most socially fruitful area of controversy. In fact, only by stressing these human realms of curiosity and imagination and inquiry can the underdeveloped societies hope to avoid in their industrialization the inhuman features of the overdeveloped—and the overdeveloped countries themselves get on the track of proper development.

VII.

THE U. S. government has quite consistently revealed an enormous fear of increased contact between its citizens and those of the Soviet bloc. The silly and insulting laws concerning fingerprinting and visas in general ought to be abolished forthwith. In this, surely, the U. S. as a free society should take the unilateral lead. It should be as convenient legally for anyone in the world to visit the United States for six months or so as it now is for a citizen of West Germany to visit Italy, or for a Swede to go to Britain. Correspondingly, all associations and individuals of the United States who wish to go any-

where in the world ought to be energetically helped to do so
by their government. The general aim, which all specific policy and action should serve, is a world without visas.

VIII.

UNDER the auspices of the United Nations, the United States
should press for and offer to share fully the costs of (1) an
international fleet of airliners for the use of scientists, intellectuals, and artists at or below cost, and (2) the construction
and maintenance of a network of simple but comfortable international centers around the world, close by universities and
libraries and laboratories, containing restaurants and sleep-
ing quarters, multilingual stenographic pools and conference
rooms of various sizes. Residence for reasonable periods of
time at these centers should be available to qualified cultural
workmen of all nationalities. And as the network expands,
qualifications for admission to these centers should be relaxed.

IX.

WASHINGTON should at once remove all security and loyalty
restrictions on scientific work and invite qualified scientists
from anywhere on the globe to participate in it. It is surely
obvious that Russians have little to learn from Americans
about the focal point of military science. But it is even more
obvious that each group has much to learn from the other,
and from all other scientific communities. It is now reasonable
to suppose that a completely free interchange of information,
technique, theory—when freely focused upon the industrial
problems of the world—would just now result in a wondrous
series of advances.

X.

THE U. S. government should immediately encourage the training of science writers, of all nationalities, who would be capable of carrying out a large-scale educational program covering such subjects as what actually goes on in "science," what it is about, what sort of projects are under way and why. Above all, these writers should be given the chance to absorb the classic ethos of science: its rules of open communication and independent dissent, its tolerance based on respect for reason, its habit of truth and of fearless observation, its demands for careful proof and its invitation to audacious speculation. For it is in this creative ethos of science and not in the gadgets of technology that the important ethical meanings of science must be sought. To make that ethics plain and to diffuse it, the serious and wonderful skills of the mass media of communication, now so largely unused or diverted to the wasteful trivialities of commercial propaganda, should be mobilized and refocused.

XI.

THE UNITED STATES government should seek to remove from the private economy all scientific research and development directly or indirectly relevant to the military. The aim should be ultimately to restrict all science and technology of any consequence to public and civilian institutions. What is needed is a public Science Machine, subject to public control. Placed within the perspective of a properly developing society, science and technology should be subjected to active public debate and control.

As a government, Washington should let no contracts of a

scientific character to any private business corporation. The principal reason for this is the old-fashioned democratic one: the simple fact that "science" is now of such public consequence that its support and its uses must be made publicly responsible. It can no longer safely be left in the hands of private powers and vested interests. There is an additional practical reason for such a policy: the wasteful cost of maintaining a Science Machine on a subsidized capitalist basis, half private, half public, split up among three armed services each with its own corporate connections and contracts.

Surely no sensible man could now object to this proposal by references to the general inefficiency and stupidity of "bureaucrats" in contrast with the efficiency and "know-how" of "businessmen." Or on the grounds that free enterprise and a free-enterprise government are necessary conditions for all scientific advance and industrial progress. Among the Russians in charge of missiles, rocketry, and all the little moons, there is not a single American businessman or free-enterprising manager; they are all "a bunch of Communistic bureaucrats" working under "a Red dictatorship" in a society only forty years removed from peasant, feudal backwardness. The truth, known to any close observer of the higher circles in America, is that most high-up American businessmen are more often than not industrially incompetent and scientifically ignorant.

XII

THE U. S. should cease all testing of nuclear devices. The Soviets have announced their unilateral suspension of such tests. Were the U. S. (and Britain) also to do so, the chance of arranging an adequate inspection system would certainly be increased. After carefully examining all the relevant scien-

tific evidence available, many physicists have concluded that
U. S. officials and scientists have been less than candid about
the hazards of fallout and the difficulty of detecting nuclear
explosions. Dr. Harry Lustig, for example, has concluded:

"There is a definite, although not yet numerically calcul-
able, danger to life from bomb testing. There is no threshold
for genetic damage; every bomb exploded, no matter how
small, takes its toll in human life. The situation is less clear
for somatic effects, such as bone cancer and leukemia, where
the possible existence of a minimum danger level may or may
not confer immunity at present fall-out levels. . . . [Nobel
Winner Linus] Pauling speaks of 15,000 seriously defective
first-generation children for each 10 megatons of fission.

"An agreement not to test any more nuclear bombs is, to a
large extent, self-enforcing; that is, violations can be detected
by monitors outside the offender's territory. . . . In order to
increase the probability of detection of all tests to where it
approaches certainty a relatively small number of inspection
stations, perhaps twenty-five, in the other power's territory
seems desirable. An agreement to establish inspection stations
would have the additional advantage of being the first break-
through in the disarmament impasse."

U. S. spokesmen should stop repeating and repeating that
all actions by the Soviets are merely "propaganda," for such
propaganda-of-the-deed as the Soviets have put out is not
merely propaganda. It is also, quite possibly, a new beginning
in the interplay of the superstates. The U. S. ought itself to
make such propaganda.

XIII.

THE U. S. government should at once and unilaterally cease
all further production of "extermination" weapons—all A-

and H-bombs and nuclear warheads included. It should announce the size of its present stockpile, along with a schedule for reducing it or converting it, so far as is technically possible, to devices for peacetime uses.

XIV.

THE government should abandon all military bases and installations outside the continental domain of the United States. It is easy to see why the Russians consider these bases as aggressive and provocative. It is as if, from the American viewpoint, Soviet bases of similar type encircled the North American continent. Examine a map of the world projected from the North Polar region, and on it, around the Western Hemisphere, locate Korea, Arabia, Japan, etc., and the point becomes immediately obvious: Bermuda, Jamaica, the tip of Alaska would be equivalent Soviet strategic-bomber bases.

XV.

THE U. S. government should encourage European nations once more to take the initiative in world history, to be the innovators, by unilaterally and immediately disarming. These nations, in particular West Germany, should renounce the whole idea of peace-by-power-of-retaliation. They should realize that their countries are now the "forward positions" of the U. S. nuclear thrust; that they are "zeroed in" as among the first targets of the Soviet thrust; that they have little, if any, power of decision over the initial blow that could end Europe as a place of human habitation; and that such a blow might well fall through human error or accident.

Were I British or German or Danish, I should demand that

my government "contract out" of NATO in its present form; I should certainly demand that the U. S. not be allowed to place in my territory launching bases for intermediate-range missiles; and I should encourage the view that the only sensible defense today is a citizens' army of riflemen. I should demand that the United States and the U.S.S.R. help to "depolarize" the world. I should accept the fact of the Oder-Neisse line as Poland's western border. I should demand of the United States and of the U.S.S.R. that both NATO and the Warsaw Pact be abandoned and that the armed forces of America be withdrawn from Europe and those of the U.S.S.R. to behind their own borders.

The general aim of a European settlement should include the amalgamation of the European economies and the establishment of a political-military status for the continent at a point somewhere between Sweden's and Austria's. I am aware that in any free reunification of Germany, East Germany would undoubtedly disappear, but this loss might not be taken too seriously by the Soviets were it part of a general European settlement of the sort I am suggesting. The Soviets have as much or more to gain from such a settlement as do Europe and America. Only by the encouragement of some such settlement in Europe could the U. S. hope to come out of the moral isolation it now occupies, in Asia as well as in Europe. For a neutralist Europe is in fact slowly coming into being. The U. S. should lead and not oppose this trend; it should become a world leader in the eyes of Europeans.

XVI.

THE U. S. government should accept the Russian proposal for an embargo on all arms shipments to the Middle East; the two powers should jointly guarantee all frontiers in the area; at the same time, with any European nations that want to co-operate, they should undertake a regional development program for the Middle East.

Western Europe needs Arabian oil; the Arabian people need Western markets for their oil. Accordingly, a Middle East Authority, under the sponsorship of the United Nations, ought to take over the oil resources and oil equipment of the region. It should sell oil on the world market at an agreed-upon price; all profits from its operations should be used to develop the Euphrates, the Tigris, the Nile, the Jordan: to make the Middle East a human landscape with an adequate standard of living for the peoples who live there. As Walter E. Packard (U. S. Chief of Land and Water Resources in Greece, 1948–54) has pointed out, such a program would benefit everyone concerned—except the feudal rulers and the present stockholders, whose rights, Mr. Packard suggests, might be purchased by the Authority.

The alternative to some such program, we already see: U. S. Marines in Lebanon, British paratroopers in Jordan, and U. S. threats to invade Iraq should the oil corporations there be threatened by the Iraqi government. The imperialist claims and actions of these corporations, and of their governments, cannot be maintained today without violence and the threat of violence. They rest upon nothing else, but they cannot for long rest upon such local violence. Western civilization began in the Middle East; the beginnings of its end could also occur there.

XVII.

THE U. S. government should at once recognize the existence of China and of all other Communist-type states; and it should seek to bring these into the world-wide economic, educational programs indicated above. This should be done not only because it is perilous not to recognize stable facts when they exist, not only because the world cannot be stabilized in peace without their inclusion, but because without what the peoples of China and India have to offer, the world is too poor to get along properly.

XVIII.

THE U. S. government should announce some such program to the world unilaterally, one big item every other day, beginning at once and in plain language. And the start should be made now. Until the sequence of announcements is completed, the U. S. government should not respond officially to inquiries from any other nation. After the announcements and actions are under way, it should earnestly seek meetings with the Russians, with or without other nations present.

The scheduling of the program should, of course, be subject to these negotiations. But first the program must be announced as a whole and definitely got under way. For that is the way to break the deadlock.

Publicly and privately, the Russians should be invited and reinvited to join in each of the efforts I have described, as well as in other projects which I am neither knowledgeable nor imaginative enough to state.

The U. S. government should now actively seek to evolve joint development plans—technical, economic, and cultural—inside each bloc, as well as among the so-called uncommitted peoples. It should, for example, strive for an exchange next year with the Soviet bloc of as many university students as facilities permit. Fifty thousand, within three years, is a suitable goal.

Let us have no nonsense about where the money is coming from. That old joke of utopian capitalism is no longer funny. The world is full of men and women; it is full of natural resources and wondrous sources of power. What is needed is the human skill and the political will to set up a new beginning. It is far less a question of money than of the kind of imagination that is at once technical and moral, the kind of mind which thinks technologically rather than in business terms. The sheer waste and fat of the overdeveloped society of the United States is by itself enough to begin with. Consider the progressive stopping up of the military ratholes of the world, the socialization of the scientific and technical apparatus of society and its world-wide release for the tasks of the human community; in half a generation we could be well on our way. The kind of problems we should then confront would be intellectually more difficult than those we now face, but we should be in a position to confront them within a more or less human world; and we should be able, with good reason, to hope that failure to solve them the first or second or third time we tried would not get us blown off the earth.

16—THE POLITICS OF PEACE

I DO not suppose that my proposals will be acted upon this week by the power elite of the United States. The anachronistic minds will not come to attention; the Secretary of State will not be tossed out in disgrace; the President will not be briefed. The small circles in East and in West which control the internecine devices will not be made responsible to any larger publics; their preparation of World War III will go on, with much secrecy, punctuated by threat and boast and probing violence; their policies will not be put to any genuinely democratic test. There will be much talk of responsible leadership, but doctrinaire and murderous rigidity will cause no ruin of reputations. The drift of events will not be seized upon and taken to the critical point of human decision. The generals will go on getting ready for what they call "the big game," assuming that they are merely doing their duty in the traditional way. The mass media will pour out their gallows humor; everyone will be very busy, their minds dominated by the commodity-ethos of the overdeveloped society. Who the hell cares about India and China and all that anyway? We got a new-model car to get out, just different enough in looks to make junk of last year's.

From their standpoint, proposals of the sort I have suggested here are indeed utopian, expensive, idealistic, unsound and, for all I know, traitorous. For the metaphysics of this elite, like that of Russia's, is the military metaphysics, and such imagination as its members possess is quite captured by military technology. We are at a curious juncture in the history of human insanity; in the name of realism, men are quite mad, and precisely what they call utopian is now the condition of human survival. Utopian action is survival action; realistic, sound, common-sense, practical actions are now the actions of madmen and idiots. And yet these men decide; these men are honored, each in his closed-up nation, as the wise and responsible leaders of our time who are doing the best they can under trying circumstances. Is it their fault that their best is not going to be good enough? Is it their fault that they've a trained incapacity to do what now ought to be done? Is it their fault that the system in which they have succeeded, and over which they fumblingly rule, is a system of semiorganized irresponsibility?

Why do not those in a position to do so throw overboard the weary old slogans with which they have stuffed their minds and take up a new line, make a new beginning? Is it that they do not really believe that war is obsolete? Is it that they really do not believe in the holocaust of World War III except as some kind of impractical bogy?

In discussing the causes of war I have given some answers to such questions, but I have delayed two answers until now because they have very much to do with the difficulties of programs for peace demanded and carried out in opposition to power elites. The first has to do with the essentially political, and so controversial, nature of peace; the second—which I shall discuss in the next chapter—with the conditions of a struggle for peace today.

Peace is such an altogether "good" word that it is well to be suspicious of it; it has meant and it does mean a great variety of things to a great variety of men. Otherwise they could not all "agree" upon it so readily and so universally. Any good word is like that; it is used by everybody, and so behind it there are hidden many political views. In the inter-war period of the twenties and thirties, "the have-nations" were all for peace—which meant the maintenance, by "legitimate force" if necessary, of the status quo in which they were paramount; "the have-not nations" were seen as trouble-makers, for they more readily viewed war as a means of what to them seemed necessary changes for "genuine peace" to prevail rather than tyranny. During World War II, Western conservatives generally meant by The Coming Peace the return of society to its prewar condition; liberals generally meant the advance and consolidation of liberal values and institutions "so that there may be no war again"; Stalinists meant the enlargement of the areas under Stalinism; militant anti-colonials understood the end of colonialism. Everybody agrees upon peace as the universal aim—and into it each packs his own specific political fears, values, hopes, demands.

This is both inevitable and proper. We cannot give to the term "peace" a definite meaning without giving it a political meaning and thus making of it a controversial term. Most of its political meanings are merely smuggled into its usage; many are stated as the conditions necessary to peace, some as the results of peace. It is possible to keep the meaning of peace pure and neutral only if we make that meaning so altogether general as to be useless in our reasoning and in our political activity.

But the key point about the political meaning of peace today is this: Before war became total, obsolete, and absurd as a means of any political and economic policy, it might have been said that peace was "a special vested interest of predominant powers," that—as E. H. Carr has put it—it was a slogan and a value by which to proclaim "an identity of interest between the dominant group [of nations] and the world as a whole . . ." But if we take seriously the nature of World War III, this political meaning of peace is no longer correct or useful. Given this kind of war, peace is no longer a cover term for ascendant nations who would preserve the status quo. As war now means the universal annihilation of man, so peace now is to the universal interests of man.

In the narrow sense, war has meant that members of one nation's population are directly and indirectly trying to kill off the population and destroy the facilities of some other nation; and that in this they are directed by elites, supported by policy-makers, and honored rather than punished by spokesmen and as well by considerable portions of the underlying public. Peace, in the narrow sense, has meant that should anyone go about killing foreigners, he would probably be punished by the elite of his own nation, publicly dishonored by his nation's spokesmen, shunned or ostracized by underlying publics.

These simple, literal, and straightforward definitions of war and peace, although useful as definitions of hot war, are no longer sufficient. Yet we should avoid smuggling into our definitions of peace any particular theories about their meanings and conditions. We ought to state the politics of peace as we see it explicitly.

War is now total; therefore, peace must now be total. The guidelines to peace I have stated are an effort to make that clear—to meet the terms of war as we now know it with the terms of peace required by the new meaning of war. We cannot, I believe, struggle for peace as we might struggle for this or for that particular reform. We cannot do so, first, because the war system is too pervasive in the leading societies of the world, and second, because the means for the struggle for peace are not now at our political disposal. Our struggle for peace, I shall argue in the next chapter, is and must be a political struggle over the very means of power required for that struggle.

In the meantime, let us be clear about this: The continued attempt by the U.S.A. to defend the economic and political status quo of the world today will end in war. To establish peace is to establish peaceful means of change, to debate their direction, and to get them under way. This, and only this, is hardheaded, realistic, sound, practical. Peaceful change requires that we adjust to the changed relations of power brought about in the world by the economic, scientific, and military success of the Soviet Union. The way to meet the challenge that this success poses is, first, to remake our own societies into properly developing ones in order that they may serve as living models of such development, and second, actively to aid underdeveloped countries, including those of the Sino-Soviet bloc, to get on such a track.

17—CONDITIONS OF

THE STRUGGLE

THE FIRST task of those who want peace is to free their imaginations from their own immediately powerless situation, in order to consider how that situation itself might be changed. If we are to struggle for peace, we must act in a democratic way in a society that is far from being altogether democratic. Our struggle for peace must at the same time be a struggle to develop and to acquire access to the means for our struggle. Our immediate and continuous fight, in short, must be a fight inside the U. S. power system over who is going to determine the uses of this nation's fabulous means of power and over the reshaping of these means into more democratically responsible instruments.

A real attack on war-making by Americans today is necessarily an attack upon the private incorporation of the economy, upon the military ascendancy, upon the linkages between the two. It requires the rehabilitation of political life,
making politics again central to decision-making and responsible to broader publics.

By democracy I mean a system of power in which those
who are vitally affected by such decisions as are made—and
as could be made but are not—have an effective voice in
these decisions and defaults. The political structure of a modern democratic state, I suggest, requires at least these six conditions:

I. It requires not only that such a public as is projected
by democratic theorists exist, but that it be the very forum
within which a politics of real issues is enacted.

II. It requires nationally responsible parties which debate
openly and clearly the issues which the nation, and indeed the
world, now so rigidly confront.

III. It requires a senior civil service firmly linked to the
world of knowledge and sensibility and composed of skilled
men who, in their careers and in their aspirations, are truly
independent of any private—that is to say, corporation—interests.

IV. It requires an intelligentsia, inside as well as outside the
universities, who carry on the big discourse of the Western
world, and whose work is relevant to and influential among
parties and movements and publics. It requires, in brief, truly
independent minds which are directly relevant to powerful
decisions.

v. It requires that there be media of genuine communication which are open to such men and with the aid of which they can translate the private troubles of individuals into public issues, and public issues and events into their meanings for the private life. This condition, as well as III and IV, are necessary if leaders are to be held responsible to publics and if there is to be an end of the divorce of the power and the intellect, an end to the higher and irresponsible ignorance, an end to the isolation of the intellect from public life.

vi. And democracy certainly requires, as a fact of power, that there be free associations linking families and smaller communities and publics on the one hand with the state, the military establishment, the corporation on the other. Unless such associations exist, there are no vehicles for reasoned opinion, no instruments for the rational exertion of public will.

Such democratic formations are not now ascendant in the power structure of the United States, and accordingly the men of decision are not men selected and formed by careers within such associations and by their performances before such publics. Accordingly, publics that do discuss issues have at most only a faint and restraining voice in the making of history, and so in the making of war or peace. To pretend that this is not so is to lose the chance to understand what is happening and why it is happening. Every step to gain these formations, these six conditions of democracy, inside the U. S. is a step toward breaking the grip of the power elite that is now set toward World War III, and a step toward making possible alternative definitions of reality and alternative policies for action.

I do not believe that these six conditions can be brought about so long as the private corporation remains as dominant and as irresponsible as it is in national and international decisions; I do not believe that they can be brought about so long as the ascendancy of the military, in personnel and in ethos, is as dominant and as politically irresponsible as it is; and certainly they cannot be brought about without filling the political vacuum that is now the key fact of U. S. politics.

Above all, the privately incorporated economy must be made over into a publicly responsible economy. I am aware of the magnitude of this task, but either we take democracy seriously or we do not. This corporate economy, as it is now constituted, is an undemocratic growth within the formal democracy of the United States. "About two-thirds of the economically productive assets of the United States, excluding agriculture," A. A. Berle, Jr., has recently calculated, "are owned by a group of not more than five hundred corporations. This is actual asset ownership. . . . But in terms of power, without regard to asset positions, not only do five hundred corporations control two-thirds of the non-farm economy, but within each of that five hundred a still smaller group has the ultimate decision-making power. This is, I think, the highest concentration of economic power in recorded history. Since the United States carries on not quite half of the manufacturing production of the entire world today, these five hundred groupings—each with its own little dominating pyramid within it—represent a concentration of power over economics which makes the medieval feudal system look like a Sunday School party." *

The corporate economy, the military ascendancy, and the political vacuum go together and support one another. One of the major reasons for their developments, I believe, is the thrust toward war, which they in turn further. Accordingly,

---

* *Economic Power and the Free Society* (Fund for the Republic, 1957).

an attack on war-making is also an attack on the U. S. power elite. An attack on this power elite is also a fight for the democratic means of history-making. A fight for such means is necessary to any serious fight for peace; it is part of that fight. Military forces and economic facilities are as much a means of history-making as is the apparatus of the state. Insofar as men want peace, they must see to it that these means are used to bring it about, that they are not made relevant to the drift and the thrust toward war. If broader publics are to make history, they must gain control of these means of history-making. To talk about peace without ever talking about the means of war is indeed to be softheaded.

The goal *and* the means of world industrial development, and so of peace, are to replace the permanent war economy by a permanent peace economy. All private profit must be taken out of the preparation for war in the U. S. economy. The economic waste of war must be taken out of the world economies. Military personnel and the military mentality must be firmly subordinated to civilian and political men and purposes. Inside the U.S.A. we must become political again.

PART FOUR—THE ROLE

OF THE

INTELLECTUALS

18—THE CULTURAL DEFAULT

INTELLECTUALS are now living in a world that drifts and is being thrust toward World War III. Both the drift and the thrust depend upon ideas: upon definitions of world reality and upon the acceptability of policies and lack of policies among elites, publics and masses. Intellectuals deal with ideas—with recollections of the past, definitions of the present, and images of possible futures. By intellectuals I mean scientists and artists, ministers and scholars; I mean those who represent the human intellect; those who are part of the great discourse of reason and inquiry, of sensibility and imagination that in the West began in Jerusalem and Athens and Rome, and that has been going on intermittently ever since. They are the organized memory of mankind, and such cultural apparatus as it has they create and they maintain. If they write, paint, speak, if they create and distribute images and ideas, their work is publicly relevant. Insofar as it is attended to, it focuses the views of men; and it distracts attention from that which it ignores. It justifies ideas of authority or it criticizes them.

Other men can feel that their power to reason, their skills to investigate, their ability to find out are inadequate to the situations they confront; they can feel that they are not expected to confront them. But intellectuals cannot. So long as they are intellectuals, they must reason and investigate and, with their passion to know, they must confront the situations of all men everywhere. That he expects this of himself is the mark of the intellectual as a type of social and moral creature. That he is alienated is another way of saying that he is capable of transcending drift, that he is capable of being man on his own.

Other men can mutter, with much justification, that they find nowhere to draw the line, to speak the emphatic "No." But it is the political and the intellectual job of the intellectual to draw just that line, to say the "No" loudly and clearly.

What scientist can claim to be part of the legacy of science and yet remain a hired technician of the military machine?

What man of God can claim to partake of the Holy Spirit, to know the life of Jesus, to grasp the meaning of that Sunday phrase "the brotherhood of man"—and yet sanction the insensibility, the immorality, the spiritual irresponsibility of the Caesars of our time?

What Western scholar can claim to be part of the big discourse of reason and yet retreat to formal trivialities and exact nonsense, in a world in which reason and freedom are being held in contempt, being smashed, being allowed to fade out of the human condition?

The answer to all these questions, if we remain generous in our conception of "cultural workmen," is quite plain: Very many scientists, very many preachers, very many intellectuals, are in default.

Scientists become subordinated parts of the Science Machines of overdeveloped nations; these machines have become essential parts of the apparatus of war; that apparatus is now among the prime causes of war; without scientists it could not be developed and maintained. Thus do scientists become helpful and indispensable technicians of the thrust toward war.

Preachers, rabbis, priests—standing in the religious default —allow immorality to find support in religion; they use religion to cloak and to support impersonal, wholesale murder —and the preparation for it. They condone the intent to murder millions of people by clean-cut young men flying and aiming intricate machineries toward Euro-Asia, zeroing in on cities full of human beings—young men who, two years before, were begging their fathers for the use of the family car for a Saturday-night date.

Intellectuals accept without scrutiny official definitions of world reality. Some of the best of them allow themselves to be trapped by the politics of anti-Stalinism, which has been a main passageway from the political thirties to the intellectual default of the apolitical fifties. They live and work in a benumbing society without living and working in protest and in tension with its moral and cultural insensibilities. They use the liberal rhetoric to cover the conservative default. They do not make available the knowledge and the sensibility required by publics, if publics are to hold responsible those who make decisions "in the name of the nation." They do not set forth reasons for human anger and give to it suitable targets.

The withdrawal of cultural workmen from politics, in

America especially, is part of the international default, which is both cultural and political, of the Western world today. The young complacents of America, the tired old fighters, the smug liberals, the shrill ladies of jingoist culture—they are all quite free. Nobody locks them up. Nobody has to. They are locking themselves up—the shrill and angry ones in the totality of their own parochial anger, the smug and complacent ones in their own unimaginative ambitions. They do not examine the U.S.A. as an overdeveloped society full of ugly waste and the deadening of human sensibility, honoring ignorance and the cheerful robot, pronouncing the barren doctrine and submitting gladly, even with eagerness, to the uneasy fun of a leisureless and emptying existence. Is not all this—our intellectual condition—among the main points our friends in Poland and Hungary, in the Soviet Union and in Yugoslavia, ought to grasp about the United States in the middle of the twentieth century? In this time of total war and of official absurdity, should not the intellectual communities of the West decide again what they are about?

Not all cultural workmen have gone the way of official conformity and intellectual default. Many, in fact, are now beginning to withdraw from the rigid military definitions of the meaning of their scientific and cultural work; they are beginning to transcend the nationalist boundaries of the contemporary mind. The meetings of scientists from both sides, arranged by Cyrus Eaton, are such a sign; the intellectual opposition to the Teller propaganda is another. Not all scientists identify science as a technological Second Coming. Not all preachers are presenting arms. Not all of them are able to comfort themselves with that sophisticated variety of theology which tells us that sin is very serious indeed, probably even original; and that accordingly we should repent mightily as we bomb. The theological tranquilizers do not quiet all urges to moral passion that Christians and humanists feel.

Among cultural workmen there is an underground revulsion from official idiocy; there is an urge to speak as cultural workmen, as scientists and scholars, as designers and ministers, to act as definers of the human condition.

Western intellectuals should remember with humility, even with shame, that the first significant crack in the cold-war front was not made by those who enjoy the formal freedom of the Western democracies, but by men who run the risk of being shot, imprisoned, driven to become nervous caricatures of human beings. The first significant cracks in the intellectual cold war came in the Communist world, after the death of Stalin. They were made not only by politicians but by professors, not only by factory workers but by writers, not only by the established but by students. They were made in Poland and Hungary and Yugoslavia, and they are still being made there. I know they are weak beginnings; that they falter and stumble. But talking in Warsaw and Zagreb and Vienna with some of those who have made the cultural break, I have seen the fingers of such men for two hours at a time continuously breaking up matchsticks on the table before them as they talk of possible new meanings of Marxism, as they try honestly to define the new beginnings in Eastern Europe after the death of Stalin. I have seen the strain and the courage, and now in the inner forum of myself those Poles and Hungarians and Yugoslavs are included. I can no longer write seriously of social and political reality without writing to them as well as to the comfortable and the safe. I can no longer write seriously without feeling contempt for the indifferent professors and smug editors of the overdeveloped societies in the West who so fearlessly fight the cold war, and for the cultural bureaucrats and hacks, the intellectual thugs of the official line who so readily have abdicated the intellect in the Soviet bloc. I can no longer write with moral surety unless I know that Leszek Kolakowski will understand where I stand —and I think this means unless he knows I have feelings of equal contempt for both leading types of underdeveloped cultural workmen of the overdeveloped countries of the world.

This is a time, I am contending, when the power of the intellectual has become potentially very great indeed. Surely there will be little disagreement among sane men that these powers are urgently needed in the construction of peaceful human societies. There is less "necessity" for more military emphasis on missiles than for moral and political imagination. There is less "need" for more Science in education than for more education in the uses of science. It is less "realistic" to spend more money on arms than to stop at once—and, if must be, unilaterally—all preparation of World War III. There is no other realism, no other necessity, no other need. If they do not mean these things, necessity and need and realism are merely the desperate slogans of the morally crippled.

War is not inevitable today; it is, immediately, the result of nationalist definitions of world reality, of dogmatic reliance upon military endeavor as the major or even the only means of solving the explosive social problems of this epoch of despair and terror. And because this is now so, to cultivate moral sensibility and to make it knowledgeable is the strategic task of those intellectuals who would be at peace. They *should* debate short-run and immediate policies, but, even more, they should confront the whole attitude toward war, they should teach new views of it, and on this basis they should criticize current policies and decisions.

Every time intellectuals have the chance to speak yet do not speak, they join the forces that train men not to be able to think and imagine and feel in morally and politically adequate ways. When they do not demand that the secrecy that makes elite decisions absolute and unchallengeable be removed, they too are part of the passive conspiracy to kill off public scrutiny. When they do not speak, when they do not demand, when they do not think and feel and act as intellectuals— and so as public men—they too contribute to the moral paralysis, the intellectual rigidity, that now grip both leaders and led around the world.

19—THE POWER AND
THE INTELLECT

WHAT are the relations of the power and the intellect in contemporary social structures—in Russia and in America? Given the human condition today, what tasks for intellectuals do these relations now make possible and urgent?

By virtue of their reason and experience, men occupying different social positions have different chances to transcend their everyday milieu and become aware of structural change. By virtue of their positions of power, men have different chances to act with history-making consequence for the structure of their society and their epoch. These two simple facts yield four types of relation of the power and the intellect:

1. Some men have the power to act with structural rele-

vance, with history-making consequence, and they are quite aware of the consequences of their actions.

II. Some men have such power but are not aware of its effective scope. Among power elites there are both types.

III. Some men, among masses and publics, cannot transcend their everyday milieus by their awareness of structure, or effect history-making change by any means of action now available to them. But there is a fourth position, which is our position:

IV. Some men are generally aware of the mechanics of history-making but clearly do not have access to the chief means of power that do exist and with which these mechanics can be influenced.

As intellectuals we *do* have one often-fragile "means of power" and it is this which provides a clue to our political role and to the political meaning of our work. It is, I think, our political task, insofar as we accept the ideal of peace— not to speak of reason and freedom—to address our work not only to ourselves but to each of the other three types of men I have classified in terms of knowledge and power:

To those with power and awareness of it, we must publicly impute varying measures of responsibility for such consequences as we find by our work to be decisively influenced by their actions and defaults. To those whose decisions have such consequences but who do not seem to be aware of them, we must assert whatever we have found out about these consequences. We must attempt to educate, and then again to impute responsibility. To those who are regularly without such power and whose awareness is confined to their everyday milieus, we must reveal by our work the meaning of structural trends and historic decisions for these milieus; we must reveal the ways in which personal troubles are connected with public issues; and in the course of these efforts, we must state what we have found out concerning the consequences of the decisions of the high and the mighty.

Any such public role for the intellectual workmen makes sense only on the assumption that the decisions and the defaults of designatable circles are now history-making; for only then can the inference be drawn that the ideas and the knowledge—and also the morality and the character—of these higher circles are immediately relevant to the human events we are witnessing. In brief, I am contending that the ideology and the lack of ideology of the powerful have become quite relevant to history-making, and that therefore it is politically relevant for intellectuals to examine it, to argue about it, and to propose new terms for the world encounter.

Attempts to avoid these troublesome issues are nowadays widely defended by the little slogan, "We are not out to save the world." Sometimes this is the disclaimer of a modest scholar; sometimes it is the cynical contempt of a specialist for all issues of larger concern; sometimes it is the disillusionment of youthful expectations; often it is the posture of men who seek to borrow the prestige of The Scientist, imagined as a pure and disembodied intellect. But sometimes it is based upon a considered judgment of the facts of power.

Because of such facts, I do not believe that intellectuals will inevitably "save the world," although I see nothing at all wrong with "trying to save the world"—a phrase which I take here to mean the avoidance of war and the rearrangement of human affairs in accordance with the ideals of human freedom and reason. But even if we think the chances dim, still we must ask: If there *are* any ways out of the crises of our epoch by means of the intellect, is it not up to intellectuals to state them?

To *appeal* to the powerful, on the basis of any knowledge we now have, is utopian in the silly sense of that term. Our relations with them are more likely to be only such relations as they find useful, which is to say that we become technicians accepting their problems and aims, or ideologists of their prestige and authority. To be more than that, so far as our political role is concerned, we must first of all reconsider the nature of our collective endeavor as intellectuals. And it is not at all utopian for one intellectual to appeal to his colleagues to undertake such a reconsideration.

Some programs are intended to be taken seriously by one or another existing party, group, or public that seems to have some chance of winning power or of immediately influencing the decisions of the powerful. Some programs are revolutionary; they are not intended for use by either of the major parties or even by smaller groups that have any reasonable hopes to seize power. There are no revolt groups of this sort in the U.S.A. today, and no hint that any may develop. There is neither constitutional nor revolutionary opposition to the existing structure of power or the types of men who run it. So neither "practical" nor "revolutionary" programs just now can very well form the serious content of all our criticisms, programs, demands.

But there is a third sense in which we may speak of political programs—a sense in which they are not intended immediately to be taken seriously either by constitutional parties or by revolutionary groups. By this third kind of program, men of independent mind attempt to formulate the conditions and the decisions necessary to realize a set of stated values or to avoid an expected disaster. It is not utopian in any useless sense, for it is not addressed directly to those in power with any expectation that they will at once take it up. Such programs, if they are any good, lay bare the structure of politics, and so today of the human condition as an object of human will and reason. They are addressed to intellectual circles and to smaller, more alert publics. So far as the powerful are concerned, such programs merely worry them; and, much more than is generally supposed, they worry their satrap opinion-makers and other supporting circles. This worry is indicated, if by nothing else, by the compulsive speed with which officials and self-appointed opinion leaders try to steal the rhetoric of such statements and twist it to the support of their going policies or lack of policies.

It is a long way around but just now it is the only way home. Many have forgotten what home is, as well as how to get there. That is one thing such programs do: They keep alive the values for which we stand. They enable us to use these values in a continual and uncompromised critique of going realities. In our situation, work on such programs is the only way to keep these values alive; if we insist upon what is called "practicality" we will surely lose touch with them, compromising them, as we accept "the lesser evil."

The intellectual's first answer to the question, "What, then, ought we to do?" is: We ought to act as political intellectuals.

In the U.S.A. today, we are not and we do not feel ourselves to be an independent force or grouping. If we are discontented or think we are discontented with the powers that be, we usually come to feel powerless, and we often fall into a merely querulous and carping sort of discourse. If we are not discontented or do not feel ourselves to be, then we usually give vague sorts of advice, generally in line with the motives and the tone of the powerful, and so we tend to become mere technicians.

But if we are to act as public intellectuals, we must realize ourselves as an independent and oppositional group. Each of us, in brief, ought to act as if he were a political party. We must act on the assumption that we are called upon to state issues, to judge men and events, to formulate policies on all major public issues. Each one of us, and all of us together, ought to feel responsible for the formulation and the setting forth of programs, even if in the beginning they are for only a few thousand readers. Politics, Lenin said, begins where there are millions. Maybe so, but it is far from the political reality of Lenin's own political life.

At just this point in human history, the role of intellectuals might well be crucial, for there is much evidence that political ideas could now become crucial. It is in terms of ideas—contained in ideologies and proclamations—that men seize upon the ends and the means supposed to be available within history and invite their pursuit and their use. A political idea is a definition of reality in terms of which decisions are formulated and acted upon by elites, accepted by masses, used in the reasoning of intellectuals. The structure of power and the role of elite decisions within it are now such as to open the way for ideas, and for their debate by publics. Ideologies and programs, arguments and critiques, handled by intellectuals, can make a difference in the shaping of our epoch and in the chances to avoid World War III.

We must remember that when, as intellectuals, we speak to and against the elite, and when we speak among ourselves, we are also speaking to such publics as may exist to overhear us. The issues of war and of peace are now of such importance, the element of decision in history-making is now so enlarged, the formal means of democratic public life are still enough available, to make it both necessary and worth while to act as if our discussion is going to make a public difference. The truth is that there has not been enough intellectual and political discussion since the thirties really to know how much effect it might have. Bipartisan foreign policy has meant no debate and no alternatives. It has meant the public and the Congressional default to executive decision. It has meant decisions in bureaucratic and expert secrecy, duly presented or "leaked" after the fact is accomplished.

If we as intellectuals, scientists, ministers do not make available, in such organs of opinion as we command, criticisms and alternatives, clearly we have little right to complain about the decline of genuine debate and about the demise of publics themselves. Given our own continued default, we cannot know what effect upon either publics or elites such public work as we might well perform and refuse to perform might have. Nobody will ever know unless we try it.

To assume such a stance as I am suggesting is to act at once politically and intellectually. And that is what is needed. To break the political monopoly of the current powers that are set toward World War III requires that their monopoly of ideas be broken. If truly independent ideas are not even formulated, if we do not set forth alternatives, then we are foolishly trapped by the difficulties those now at the top have got us into. They do not want us to identify *their* difficulties as theirs; they want us to think of *their* difficulties as if these were everybody's. That is what they call "constructive thinking about public problems."

What *they* want they call "constructive," but there are no constructive ways out of their bankruptcy. To be constructive in their sense is merely to stick our heads further into their sack. So many of us have already stuck our heads in there that our first job is to pull them out and look around again for genuine alternatives. In this sense it must be said: the first job of the intellectuals today is to be consistently and altogether unconstructive. For to be constructive within the going scheme of affairs is to consent to the continuation of precisely what we ought to be against.

20—GUIDELINES, II

IN PART THREE I suggested some guidelines to a general program for peace. In this chapter I am concerned with specific ways open, in this time of total war and crackpot realism, to intellectuals who want peace. When we search for ways to peace, as I have already indicated, we immediately come up against the fact that the struggle for peace is also an ideological struggle over the meaning of peace, and as well a political struggle over the very means of the struggle itself. In what follows I shall try to take these problems of power into account as I suggest several things which intellectuals can and should immediately set about doing.

I.

THE PASSION to define the reality of the human condition in an adequate way and to make our definitions public—that is the guideline to our work as a whole. It is our first task as an intellectual community publicly to confront the new facts of history-making and so of political responsibility and irresponsibility. It is our job continually to investigate the causes of World War III, and to locate among those causes the responsibility for decisions and defaults in any and all nations. In slowly drifting periods of man's history, it was possible that leaders be mediocrities and no one know it or care: What great difference did it make? But in periods which are neither slow nor necessarily drifting, the fact is that leaders may very well make all the difference between life and death. That point we must make into an insistent and clear-cut issue of U. S. politics. We must debunk the ideological proclamations that support faulty decisions, and expose the dogmatic assumptions upon which they rest. We must fight against the doctrine that "we" are in the sack, that there are no alternatives, that any other line of thought and action than the one now being followed is utopian and impractical.

II.

WE MUST release the human imagination, in order to open up a new exploration of the alternatives now possible for the human community; we must set forth general and detailed plans, ideas, visions; in brief, programs. We must transcend the mere exhortation of general principle and opportunist reactions. What are needed are commanding views of the future, and it is our opportunity and our task to provide them. We must develop and debate among ourselves—and then among larger publics—genuine programs; we must make of these programs *divisive* and *partisan* political issues within the U.S.A.

We are not merely upholders of standards; we are also creators of standards. And we must realize that the capacity to formulate radical views and higher standards is an advantage which the alienation that intellectuals enjoy and suffer makes available to them. The exercise of such freedom is at once a great advantage of such "alienation" and a prime and felicitous use of it. Among us now "alienation" is often a whining little slogan of escape; it ought to be a seized opportunity. When we decry, as we should, the loss of standards and the deterioration of aspirations, we should also set forth new standards, or we are falling down on our proper job. Without commanding views of the future, we do not have appropriate criteria by which to judge events and decisions or the main drift in which the interplay results. Without audacious programs, without insistent debate, we cannot hope to orient ourselves, or such publics as we may find and help to create, to the realities of the world encounter and to the possible meanings of peace.

III.

WE SHOULD take democracy seriously and literally. Insofar as we accept the democratic heritage—as not only our heritage but as of use and of value to the world tomorrow—we must realize that it has been a historically specific formation, brought about by a set of factors, a union of procedural devices and ideological claims quite specific to Western civilization; and that it is now in a perilous condition not only in the world but in the West itself, and especially in the United States of America. In the U. S. we must begin insistently to make that peril clear; we must clarify again the values that are threatened, and the trends and decisions that now threaten them; and we must consider and invent programs by which the threat can be lessened, the chances of the values to be realized maximized. The thing to do with civil liberties is to use them. The thing to do within a formal democracy is to act within it and so to give it content. If we do not do so, then we ought to stop "defending" democracy and say outright that we do not take it seriously.

IV.

WHAT WE, as intellectuals, ought to do with the formal means of communication—in which so many now commit their cultural default—is to use them as we think they ought to be used, or not to use them at all. We should assume that these means are among *our* means of production and work; that they have been arbitrarily expropriated from us, privately and illegitimately incorporated; and that they are now being used for stupid and corrupting purposes, which disgrace us before the world and before ourselves. We should claim these means as important parts of our means of cultural endeavor, and we should attack those among us who prostitute their talents and disgrace us as an intellectual community. We should write and speak for the mass media on our own terms or not at all. We should attack those who allow themselves to be used by them merely for money or merely for prestige. We should make the mass media the means of liberal—which is to say, liberating—education.

V.

WE MUST remember that political indifference is to some extent part and parcel of an affluent society, of a rich society in full prosperity. But we must not forget that the U. S. is subject to slump as well as to boom, and that no one knows what the psychology of the unemployed man in mid-century America is going to be, nor what political direction, if any, it may take. We ought as intellectuals to try to find out this psychology and these possible directions; and we ought by our work to try to inform it and to shape its directions.

Slump is no more a matter of fate than is war. Slump is a man-made disaster, and, as I have already suggested, the two disasters—slump and war—are connected. We ought to connect them in the public mind. We must not allow measures to alleviate slump, ways to subsidize the defaults of the capitalist economy, to be entangled with the means of war and the push toward World War III. As economists we ought carefully to build dramatic models of the U. S. economy with the economics of war subtracted from them, for then the role of war in this economy and of the economic causes of war would become open to inspection. We ought to work out measures to avoid slump without preparing for war in order that they might be publicly demanded. We should, in brief, *confront* capitalism as one type of political economy and—in view of the economic mechanics of slump and war—we ought to debate alternatives to it.

VI.

No ONE knows what the public effects might be were U. S. senators, even a handful of them, to investigate fully and in detail the economics and the politics of the drift and the thrust toward World War III. It is the most sinister and disastrous effect of McCarthyism that it has given the term "Senate investigation" such an ugly and irresponsible sound. But intellectuals should remember that the one solid power still in the hands of legislative bodies is the power to investigate the corporate, the military, the political bureaucracies. By our intellectual work and by our political demands, we ought to encourage senators to think nationally and internationally rather than only about their sovereign localities. We ought to encourage them and to help them to use the power of the Senate to investigate the causes of World War III and to formulate policies for peace and for its conditions. We ought to encourage them and help them to examine the corporate world of business, the business world of government, and the corporate and political realms of the military establishment—in short, the power elite in its each and every implication for democracy, for peace, for properly developing societies. No private intellectual can do this adequately; it requires the senatorial power of subpoena. But it also requires intellectual demand and support and work. It requires that the research of social scientists be focused upon important issues, rather than—with whatever formal ingenuity—upon precise trivialities.

VII.

ONE PITIFUL objection to the assumption of such a role as I am outlining is that as intellectuals we could not get the information needed to act and to speak in an informed way, for so much of it is now secret. This objection we must turn into nonsense. Even in scientific and military fields, the plea of ignorance is often more an easy excuse than a vital fact. Moreover, if those in power keep secret information relevant to policy issues, it is precisely the intellectuals who ought to demand that they tell it. There are many ways to make such demands effective. One of them, for example, is to assume the range of possible answers now kept secret, and to speculate audaciously about each of them. That is very worrisome. Another is continually to confront the secrecy-mongers with their own rhetoric of free discussion. These are not futile tasks; they are ways to make firm the now weak and inarticulate public. They are ways by which those who are articulate can become rallying points of oppositional opinion and independent judgment.

We must demand full information of relevance to human destiny, and the end of decisions made in irresponsible secrecy.

VIII.

WHAT IS required of us, as intellectuals, in short, is that *we* stop fighting the cold war of self-co-ordinated technicians and hired publicists, of self-appointed spokesmen, of pompous scientists who have given up the scientific ethos for the ethos of war technology. We must cease being intellectual dupes of political patrioteers. This disgraceful cold war is surely a war in which we as intellectuals ought at once to become conscientious objectors. To make that decision does not even require great risk or self-sacrifice. It requires only sanity and getting on with our proper job.

IX.

PART OF that job is personally to try, again and again, to make contact with our opposite numbers among those now officially defined as our enemy, and to enable and encourage them to make contact with us.

Instead of going on publicity junkets to SAC bases, officially and conveniently arranged, we ought to go on our own, if necessary, and no matter how difficult, on intellectual and human expeditions to China, to Eastern Europe, to Russia. And we should request and demand that this intellectual travel be made easy and convenient.

When we are on exchange programs as students and as professors outside America, we ought not to feel that we are semiofficial representatives of any country. We ought to know that we represent intellectual and cultural values that are not confined by any nationalist boundary. If other minds are captive—and many are—we must show them, we must reveal how an uncaptured mind works.

When we reach our opposite numbers among the enemy, we ought first to speak with them informally and in direct human terms. We should tell them how we actually work and live as intellectuals, scientists, artists, in detail and in full autobiographical candor. And we should ask such questions of them. From that we ought to move into the exchange of ideas about programs.

With them, we ought to make our own separate peace.

As intellectuals, and so as public men, ought we not to act and work as if this peace, and the interchange of values, programs and ideas of which it consists, is everybody's peace, or surely ought to be? As Americans, we might realize the place in the world of the power of this nation, and we might take upon ourselves the responsibility of stating how it is being used and how we believe it ought to be used. As intellectuals of the world we should awake and unite with intellectuals everywhere.

X.

As INTELLECTUALS, we use our own skills in the analysis of human affairs and the development and expression of ideas about them. We ought now to use these skills in an effort to speak to our colleagues, among whom two groups are especially relevant, even strategic, to stopping the thrust toward World War III and getting on the road to peace: ministers of God and physical scientists.

21—A PAGAN SERMON

To UNDERSTAND the pivotal decisions of our times, it is not necessary to consider religious institutions or personnel or doctrine as independent forces. Neither preachers nor the religious laity matter; what they do and what they say can be readily agreed with and safely ignored. By most of those who do matter, and those who do decide, it is taken as irrelevant Sunday chatter, or it is used as an instrument of their own altogether secular purposes. Wherever religion does count, it is used. In Europe, for example, what is still called "Catholicism" is well united with provincial U. S. policy. From Franco's Spain to Adenauer's Germany, the American use of Catholicism, and vice versa, to turn Europe into an integrated and loyal launching pad seems quite successful.

I am aware that there are exceptions: The Quakers remain firm; and small groups and individuals everywhere stand up on religious principles to confront political immorality and ir-responsibility. But the average ministerial output is correctly heard as a parade of worn-out phrases. It is generally unim-aginative and often trivial. As public rhetoric, it is boring and irrelevant. As private belief, it is without passion. In the world of the West, religion has become a subordinate part of the overdeveloped society.

I.

As A social and as a personal force, religion has become a de-pendent variable: It does not originate; it reacts. It does not de-nounce; it adapts. It does not set forth new modes of conduct and sensibility; it imitates. Its rhetoric is without deep appeal; the worship it organizes is without piety. It has become less a revitalization of the spirit in permanent tension with the world than a respectable distraction from the sourness of life. Well settled among the nationalist spokesmen, the verbal output of U. S. religious leaders is now part of the defining of reality that is official, rigid, and inhuman. In a quite direct sense, religion in America has generally become part of the false consciousness of the world and of the self.

Among the cheerful robots of the mass society, not human virtue but human shortcomings, attractively packaged, lead to popularity and success. These robots are men and women without publicly relevant consciousness, without awareness of shocking human evil, and their religion is the religion of good cheer and glad tidings. That it is a religion without dreary religious content is less important than that it is socially brisk and that it is not spiritually unsettling. It is a getting chummy with God, as a means to quite secular good feelings.

With such religion, ours is indeed a world in which the idea of God is dead. But what is important is that this fact itself is of no felt consequence. In brief, men and women are religiously indifferent; they find no religious meanings in their lives and in their world. They do not base their hopes or their fears upon any such meaning. For them religious symbols have lost their effectiveness as motives for personal conduct and as justifications for public policy. Whatever malaise and exaltation, whatever bewilderment and orientation, most men now know have little to do with religion. They are neither proreligious nor antireligious; they are simply areligious.

The verbal Christian belief in the sanctity of human life has not been affected by the impersonal barbarism of twentieth-century war. But this belief does not itself enter decisively into the plans now being readied for World War III. Stalin once asked how many divisions the Pope had, and it was a relevant question. No one need ask how many chaplains there are in any army that wants them; there are as many as the generals and their satraps feel the need of. Religion has become a willing spiritual means and a psychiatric aide of the nation-state. Nationalism is today the world's idolatrous religion. Moreover, as nations are more and more obviously dealers in violence governed by expediency, more and more do religious leaders bless their calculations for disaster and their expedient lies.

Total war ought indeed to be difficult for the Christian conscience to confront, but the current Christian way out makes it easy; war is defended morally and Christians easily fall into line—as they are led to justify it—in each nation in terms of Christian faith itself. Men of religious congregations do evil. Ministers of God make them feel good about doing it. Rather than guide them in the moral cultivation of their consciences, ministers, with moral nimbleness, blunt that conscience, covering it up with peace of mind.

To say that these times are corrupt *because* they are idolatrous is to be arrogant about the casual weight of religious
creeds; to define the world struggle as a struggle between
"religious" and "atheistic" forces, as Dulles has continually
done, is surely mere uninformed bigotry. On both sides,
among leaders and among led, there are atheists as well as
members of all the world's religions—and also many hypo-
crites, religious and otherwise. Because men are heretical does
not mean they are necessarily immoral. The official religious
definition of the cold war is an entrapment of the Christian
conscience.

II.

THE MORAL death of religion in the U.S.A. is inherent neither
in religion nor specifically in Christianity. At times this religion
has been insurgent, at other times complacent; and it has been
characterized by repeated revivals. Just now it is neither
revolutionary nor reactionary, and it makes no real effort to
revive itself in order to examine the issues of publics and the
troubles of individuals from a fresh religious perspective. It
does not count in the big political balance of life and death.

This is not surprising; in fact, it is readily explainable. In
their struggle for success, religious institutions have come into
competition with great contemporary forces, primarily amusement and politics, and, in higher circles, scientific rationalism.
Each of these has been winning over religion; and when religion has seemingly won over them, it has failed as religion.

The most obvious competition is with the world of industrialized entertainment. Competing with these mass means of
distraction, churches have themselves become minor institu-

tions among the mass media of communication. They have imitated and borrowed the strident techniques of the insistent publicity machines, and in the terms of the pitchman (with both the hard and the soft sell) they have made banal the teachings, indeed the very image, of Christ.

I do not believe that anything recognizably Christian can be conveyed in this way. This religious malarkey diseducates the congregation exposed to it; it kills off any real influence religious leaders might have. Even if the crowds come, they come only for the show; and if it is the nature of crowds to come, it is also their nature soon to go away. And in all truth, are not the television Christians in reality armchair atheists? In value and in reality they live without the God they profess; despite ten million Bibles sold each year in the United States, they are religiously illiterate. Neither their lives nor their thoughts are informed by the creeds they say they believe to be the revealed word. "If Christ had been put on television to preach the Sermon on the Mount," Malcolm Muggeridge has recently written, "viewers would either have switched onto another channel, or contented themselves with remarking that the speaker had an interesting face. Christ might have become a television personality, but there would have been no Christianity."

To ministers of God we must now say: If you accept the entertainment terms of success, you cannot succeed. The very means of your "success" make for your failure as witnesses, for you must appeal to such diverse moral appetites that your message will necessarily be generalized to the point of moral emptiness. If you do not specify and confront real issues, what you say will surely obscure them. If you do not alarm anyone morally, you will yourself remain morally asleep. If you do not embody controversy, what you say will inevitably be an acceptance of the drift to the coming human hell. On the road to that hell everyone may vote for you, but that vote will be meaningless. You will be less a lively center than a dead end. Continuing to live with the convenient ambiguities of gospel, you may think you are a reasonably compromising institution; in fact you will be a compromised faith, and in the end your religious contentment will be neither religious nor contented. And in all this you will continue the characteristic history of Christianity, for the Christian record *is* rather clear: From the time of Constantine to the time of global radiation and the uninterceptible missile, Christians have killed Christians and been blessed for doing so by other Christians.

Politics, like religion, has also come into competition with and been deeply influenced by the world of entertainment and its means of attraction and distraction. But the realities of politics and economics are nowadays very difficult to ignore; they just won't down. Moreover, they are indispensable to the military organization of society. Religion cannot compete with the political and military perils. What vision of hell compares with the realities we now confront? And the point is that ministers of God are not foremost among those few men who would define and expose the morality of the political decisions and indecisions that lie back of these morally atrocious events and preparations. For a church whose congregation contains all political views and which is out for statistical success feels it must prosperously balance "above" politics— which means that it serves whatever moral default the affairs of mankind reveal.

As a mass medium, religion has become a religiously ineffective part of the show that fills up certain time slots in the weekly routine of cheerful robots. As an institution that is part of a political society, religion has become a well-adapted rear guard. Rather than denounce evil, rather than confront agony, the minister goes his amiable way, bringing glad tidings into each and every home.

III.

To such ministers secular intellectuals ought to deliver pagan sermons, my own version of which is as follows:

Gentlemen: Since we are among those pagans who take declarations seriously, we must ask you, as declared Christians, certain questions.

What does it mean to preach? Does it not mean, first of all, to be religiously conscious? We do not see how you can preach unless as a man you are the opposite to the religiously indifferent. To be religiously conscious, we suppose, is to find some sort of religious meaning in one's own insecurities and desires, to know oneself as a creature in some kind of relation with God which increases your hope that your expectations and prayers and actions will be realized. We must ask: For you today what is that religious meaning?

To preach, secondly, means to serve as a moral conscience and to articulate that conscience. We do not see how you can do that by joining the publicity fraternity and the weekend crusaders. You cannot do it by "staying out of politics." You are up against the competition with amusement and the competition with politics, and we think there is only one way in which you can compete as religious men with religious effect: Each of you must be yourself in such a way that your views are unmistakably from you as a moral center. From that center of yourself you must speak. So we must ask: Why do you not make of yourself the pivot, and of your congregation the forum, of a public that is morally directed and that is morally standing up? The Christian ethic cannot be socially

incorporated without compromise; it can only live in a series
of individuals who are capable of morally incorporating it in
themselves.

Do not these times demand a little Puritan defiance? Do not
they demand the realization of how close hell is to being a
sudden and violent reality in man's world today? Should not
those who still have access to the peoples of Christendom
stand up and denounce with all the righteousness and pity
and anger and charity and love and humility their faith may
place at their command the political and the militarist assumptions now followed by the leaders of the nations of Christendom? Should they not denounce the pseudoreligiosity of men
of high office who would steal religious phrases to decorate
crackpot policies and immoral lack of policies? Should they
not refuse to repeat the official, un-Christian slogans of dull
diplomats who do not believe in negotiation, who mouth
slogans which are at most ineffective masks for lack of policy?
Should they not realize that the positive moral meaning of
what is called "neutralism" lies in the resolve that the fate of
mankind shall not be determined by the idiotically conducted
rivalry of the United States and the Soviet Union?

We do not wish to be politically dogmatic, but merely brief,
and, as you gentlemen surely have recognized, we are religiously illiterate and unfeeling. But truly we do not see how
you can claim to be Christians and yet not speak out totally
and dogmatically against the preparations and testings now
under way for World War III. As we read it, Christian doctrine in contact with the realities of today cannot lead to any
other position.

You will not find in moral principles the solution to the
problems of war, but without moral principles men are
neither motivated nor directed to solve them. Moral principles
are often unachievable, but that is nothing against them; they
are guides and canons, not visible and disposable consumer

goods. But nowadays we pagans see that Christian morals are more often used as moral cloaks of expedient interests than ways of morally uncloaking such interests.

In the end, we believe the decisive test of Christianity lies in your witness of the refusal by individuals and by groups to engage in war. Pacifism, we believe, is the test of your Christianity—and of you. At the very least, it ought to be *the* debate within Christendom.

The brotherhood of man is now less a goal than an obvious condition of biological survival. Before the world is made safe again for American capitalism or Soviet communism or anything else, it had better be made safe for human life.

What have you to say to the peoples of Indonesia, Russia, China? When you preach do you imagine they are in your church or temple and speak to them? If not, what to you is the meaning of the brotherhood of man?

But you may say, "Don't let's get the church into politics." You might well say that with good conscience were the political role of the church to be confined to what it has been and what it is. But in view of what it might be, if you say that you are saying, "Don't let's get the church into the world; let's be another distraction from reality." This world *is* political. Politics, understood for what it really is today, has to do with the decisions men make which determine how they shall live and how they shall die. They are not living very well, and they are not going to die very well either. Politics is the locale of both evil and of good. If you do not get the church into politics, you cannot confront evil and you cannot work for good. You will be a subordinate amusement and a political satrap of whatever is going. You will be the great Christian joke.

Men and ideas, the will and the spirit, are now being tested, perhaps in all truth for the final time; and in this testing so far, you Christians are standing in default. The key sign of this is the fact of your general lack of effective opposition, of your participation in the fact of moral insensibility. That, of course, is a world fact about publics and masses and elites, but it is all the more grievous among Christians, if only because of the expectations that they have aroused about themselves. Yet who among you has come out clearly and unambiguously on the issues of internecine war and the real problems of peace?

Who among you is considering what it means for Christians to kill men and women and children in ever more efficient and impersonal ways?

Who among you uses his own religious imagination to envision another kind of basis for policies governing how men should treat with one another?

Who among you, claiming even vague contact with what Christians call "The Holy Spirit," is calling upon it to redeem the day because you know that the times are evil?

If you are not today concerned with this—the moral condition of those in your spiritual care—then, gentlemen, what *is* your concern? As pagans who are waiting for your answer, we merely say: You claim to be Christians. And we ask: What does that mean as a biographical and as a public fact?

In moral affairs you are supposed to be among the first of men. No moral affair today compares with the morality of warfare and the preparation for it, for in these preparations men usurp—as you might say—the prerogatives of God. By sitting down and by keeping quiet, by all too often echoing the claptrap of the higher immorality that now passes for political leadership, you are helping to enfeeble further in this time of cruel troubles the ideals of your founder. Christianity is part of the moral defeat of man today. Perhaps it is no longer important enough to be considered a cause of it;

perhaps it is only among the passive doctrines of the spectators of man's moral defeat.

I hope you do not merely demand of me gospels and answers and doctrines and programs. According to your belief, my kind of man—secular, prideful, agnostic and all the rest of it—is among the damned. I am on my own; you've got your God. It is up to you to proclaim gospel, to declare justice, to apply your love of man—the sons of God, all of them, you say—meaningfully, each and every day, to the affairs and troubles of men. It is up to you to find answers that are rooted in ultimate moral decision and to say them so that they are compelling.

I hope your Christian conscience is neither at ease nor at attention, because if it is I must conclude that it is a curiously expedient and ineffective apparatus. I hope you do not believe that in what you do and in how you live you are renouncing evil, because if you do, then I must infer that you know nothing of evil and so nothing of good. I hope you do not imagine yourselves to be the bearers of compassion, because if you do, you cannot yet know that today compassion without bitterness and terror is mere girlish sentiment and not worthy of a full-grown man. I hope you do not speak from the moral center of yourselves, because if you do, then in the dark nights of your soul, in fear and in trembling, you must be cruelly aware of your moral peril in this time of total war, and—given what you, a Christian, say you believe—I, a pagan, pity you.

22—SCIENCE AND SCIENTISTS

WITHIN the internationalism of science, the nations of Western Europe have occupied a more central place than has the United States or the Soviet Union. In part, this has been due to their historical lead and in part to the fact that in Europe science has been an integral part of the broader European cultural tradition. Historically, America and Russia have stood as provincials to Western Europe in matters of theoretical innovation in basic science.

U. S. science has not developed a firm scientific tradition in the European manner. Here science has been virtually identified with its technological products, its engineering developments, its techniques; and it has recently become subjected to the corporate technique of the assembly line. It is in the use of science, in the know-how of development projects, in the mass-production exploitation of its legacy, that the U. S. has excelled. This kind of industrial and military science stands in contrast to the classic, academic tradition in which individual scientific investigators or small groups are part of an un-co-ordinated cultural tradition. In brief, the U. S. has built a Science Machine: a corporate organization and rationalization of the process of technological development and to some extent—I believe unknown—of scientific discovery itself.

It is to the engineering "crash program," made possible by the Science Machine, that U. S. science has been increasingly geared. And it is in just this respect that the Soviet Union has at first imitated and now, it would seem, overtaken the United States.

In both superstates, the incentive and the climax of such a development are making of science a firm and managed part of the machinery of war. It is true that Russia is unhampered by the wasteful character of a Science Machine subjected to private capitalist profit. More easily than the U. S. elite, the Soviet elite can probably focus her science upon basic or upon immediately technological purposes. But under the cold-war pressure, the overriding aim of both is a Science Machine geared to the war machine. In Russia as well as in America, accordingly, scientists are viewed as a vital national resource; tight secrecy is demanded of scientists; many who would be scientists are converted into engineering types. The scientist, in short, is to be a unit of the Science Machine; the Science Machine, in turn, is to be managed by nonscientific personnel or by new types of managerial scientists. The ethos of basic science and the role of the creative individual—as they have been known in Western civilization—are violated by the construction and the maintenance of military Science Machines, in the U. S. version of which over one third of creative scientists are now deeply and directly involved.

It should not be supposed that American scientists have not reacted to all this, or to the uses to which the fearful products of the Science Machine have been put and the uses now officially planned. On the issue of the bomb, scientists have probably been more politically conscious than any other professional group. It is true that their initial reactions and influence following World War II were greatly blunted by official action in the case of J. Robert Oppenheimer and by the dissolution of the wartime Office of Scientific Research and Development. Still, a significant number of scientists quietly refuse to do weapons work; many more are active enough in "the campaign to stop the testing of bombs" to circulate and to sign petitions. Many scientists, moreover, have fought hard against the excesses of the "security program"; they have demanded that materials be declassified, and that "top secret" restrictions upon human knowledge be removed.

The power of science to change the world has increased; but the influence of scientists over the Science Machines has become a public issue. For scientists, that issue is not merely the position they will take on the cold war or even whether as individuals they will work on the new weaponry. It is not merely a question of basic versus applied science. Behind these issues and others like them is the contradiction of the classic scientific ethos by the Science Machine. The issue is basic science as part of a cultural tradition of international scope versus the nationalist, secret Science Machine.

Especially among younger scientists in the United States (I do not know about the Soviet Union in this respect) scientists are becoming more fully aware of what it means to work in the one or in the other; of the fact that as scientists they are part of a broader tradition which includes the humanities and the liberal arts; of the difference between scientists who are necessarily in and of this broader tradition and technologists and engineers who are not necessarily a part of it at all; of the fact that within the Science Machine certain types of scientists are rising who know nothing of the classic ethos of science. Within the scientific community, in brief, there has come about a split which scientists increasingly feel called upon to confront.

I.

THE FIRST thing scientists should do is join the intellectual community more fully than they have and, as members, take up with other cultural workmen the tasks I have been outlining. They should develop and work to fulfill a program for peace. More specifically: They should attempt to deepen the split among themselves and to debate it.

II.

SCIENTISTS OF all nations ought to honor publicly those of their colleagues who have already made their declarations for peace and against the war of the Science Machines. As scientists and as cultural workmen they ought to be gladdened by the courage displayed by such men as the eighteen German physicists who have made their declarations against working on the new weaponry. A West German spokesman recently said, "The possibility of a veto by the Eighteen still hangs like a sword of Damocles over all government decisions concerning defense policy." And Robert Jungk has written: "It even seems that the fear of the uproar that might be roused by a second declaration by the atomic scientists has again and again forced the Bonn Government to camouflage and even revise its armament and foreign policy programs."

III.

SCIENTISTS OF all nations ought to declare against those among them who, as scientists, make their calling, in the words of Norman Cousins, "seem more mysterious than it is, and who allow this mystery to interfere with public participation in decisions involving science or the products of science." They ought, as Harrison Brown has recently done, to declare against those individual scientists who lend their prestige and their official names to the program for war undertaken by governments. They should point out the position and the prestige which, inside the iron wall of secrecy, enable some scientists to make pronouncements which cannot be checked or refuted by critics. Scientists should not lend their authority to the propaganda output of the A.E.C. or to Presidential assertion. More of them ought, on appropriate occasion, to make such statements as this one by Harrison Brown: "I believe that Dr. Teller is willfully distorting the realities of the situation, I believe that it is possible for us to secure agreements with the Soviet Union to stop tests, and I believe further that the agreements could be of such a nature that the Soviet Union would adhere to them because it would be very much to her advantage to do so."

IV

SCIENTISTS should establish their own private forums and public outlets. For the time is overripe for an intensified and responsible communication between scientists and other cultural workmen, and between scientists and larger publics. When scientific answers are needed to clarify questions of public policy but are not known, after consultation with one another scientists should admit this. When answers are known, they should publicize them responsibly as scientists. In short, they ought informally but professionally to constitute themselves a politically neutral but politically relevant "higher civil service." Only in some such way can they avoid irresponsible controversies among themselves and avoid being used by officials and warlords who would lie and bluff for their own ends. Only in some such way can they avoid establishing themselves before publics as hired men of ruling circles, and come to be seen as members of the cultural community, and so responsible to mankind.

V.

The scientists' debate ought to result in the development of a code of ethics for scientists. Just as lawyers and doctors become aware of their deep social involvement, set up a code of professional ethics, so now should scientists. The purpose of such a code among any professional group is to protect the practitioners from each other and from other groups; often the code is no more than that. But it ought also to protect society from unethical practices of the practitioners, and of course to define such practices. Philip Siekovitz—a biochemist and medical researcher—has recently proposed such a code for scientists. Its purpose, he suggests, is not "to govern society, but only to assist in the self-regulation of individuals; it would serve not for the control of research, but for the maintenance of standards. Psychologists have no business helping some groups fashion keys for opening, surreptitiously, the pocketbooks of others. Medical scientists, chemists, and bacteriologists have no business working for the special interests of some against the interests of the many. These men are no longer scientists; they are technicians in the employ of men with exclusive interests. What we need is a kind of guild system in science which would exclude such technicians from the practice of research. . . ."

One of the great yields of any attempt by scientists to formulate such a code and to enforce it among themselves would be the furthering of moral and political debate within the scientific community.

VI.

OUT OF such debate one might also hope that the demand would arise for the establishment of a civilian "Department of Science and Technology." All scientific agencies of the government should be placed in this department, which should become the focal point of the scientists' effort as scientists and as cultural workmen aware of their political role. To replace the present labyrinth and confusion of committees and consultants by such a centralized organization would increase the chance for a responsible public role of science and scientists. It would constitute a forum within which debates about science and policy debates by scientists could be made democratically open and responsible. And it would increase the chance that scientific endeavor would be removed from military authority and Pentagon decision.

VII.

SCIENTISTS AS scientists and as members of the cultural community ought not, I believe, to encourage or aid the U. S.

elite to straighten out its Science Machine in order to catch up with and overtake the U.S.S.R.'s. They ought not to worry about the United States' science lag as such. They ought to use that worry to spur reflection about the uses of scientific rationality in both the U. S. and the U.S.S.R. The scientific community ought to debate, and to encourage among wider publics the debate, as to whether, given the human community and the world's resources, scientific work and technological development are being responsibily focused.

They ought, for example, publicly to ask and to ask themselves: Who wants to go to the moon anyway? Do you? Really? Aren't there other things you'd much rather do? And however you feel, do you realize that an increasing part of your life effort is being spent on just this kind of little trip— at an increasing risk to your life?

I am less concerned that any one point of view on this prevail than that the decisions involved be made public issues and, as such, debated by publics and by cultural workmen before publics. I am concerned that the human exploration of space be placed in the context of a properly developing society, rather than in that of the military metaphysic.

My own view, however, is that only those who make a fetish of Scientific Progress, irrespective of its direction and result, would today think the emphasis on space travel a reasonable and proper use of man's rationality, effort, and resources. Given its military bearing and the military perils on which it rests and which it increases, it is an irrational focus for such total scientific effort. And given the human condition today, it is an immoral expenditure of economic energy. But as a climactic step in an irresponsible series of decisions and defaults, it fits very well the military metaphysic which possesses the crackpot elites of Russia, the United States, and points in between.

VIII.

SCIENTISTS should demand that all security and loyalty restrictions be removed from all scientific work, and that qualified scientists anywhere on the globe—specifically and immediately including J. Robert Oppenheimer—be invited to participate in it. They should make it clear that there is no security in "scientific secrecy," that such secrecy leads to anxiety and fear, to nervous officials and to official nervousness; that secrecy leads only to insecurity.

To those who accuse them of "defeatism" or of "favoring Soviet armament" they ought to reply in the words of the German physicist, Max von Laue: "Suppose I live in a big apartment house and burglars attack me; I am allowed to defend myself and, if need be, I may even shoot, but under no circumstances may I blow up the house. It is true that to do so would be an effective defense against burglars, but the resulting evil would be much greater than any I could suffer. But what if the burglars have explosives to destroy the whole house? Then I would leave them with the responsibility for the evil, and would not contribute anything to it."

IX.

As CONSCIOUS members of the cultural community, scientists ought to work within their scientific tradition and refuse to become members of a Science Machine under military authority. Within the civilian Department of Science, within their profession, and before larger publics, they should publicly defend and practice science in terms of its classic, creative ethos, rather than in terms of the gadgets of the overdeveloped society or the monstrous weapons of the war machines. They should demand that a free interchange of information and theory be focused upon the industrial problems of the world. For reasons I have already given, they ought, with other cultural workmen, to seek to remove scientific research and development directly or indirectly relevant to the military from the private economy. They should contend that Washington let no contracts of a scientific character to any private business corporation. As a profession they should debate the refusal to work under such contracts and consider the professional boycotting of given projects. In passive and in active ways, they ought unilaterally to withdraw from, and so abolish, the Science Machine as it now exists.

"But if I don't do it," some scientists feel, "others will. So what's the difference?" This is less an argument than the mannerism of the irresponsible. It is based upon a conception of yourself as an altogether private man, upon the acceptance of your own impotence, upon the idea that the act in question, whatever it be, is part of fate and so not subject to your decision.

My answers to this mannerism are: If you do not do it, you at least are not responsible for its being done. If you refuse to do it out loud, others may quietly refrain from doing it, and those who still do it may then do it only with hesitation and guilt. To refuse to do it is to begin the practice of a professional code, and perhaps the creation of that code as a historical force. To refuse to do it is an act affirming yourself as a moral center of responsible decision; it is an act which recognizes that you as a scientist are now a public man—whether you want to be or not; it is the act of a man who rejects "fate," for it reveals the resolution of one human being to take at least his own fate into his own hands.

23—ON FATE AND THE

RADICAL WILL

WHAT I have been trying to say to intellectuals, preachers, scientists—as well as more generally to publics—can be put into one sentence: Drop the liberal rhetoric and the conservative default; they are now parts of one and the same official line; transcend that line.

There is still a good deal of talk, so fashionable several years ago, about the collapse of "right" and "left"; about "conservative" and "radical" being no longer viable as intellectual and political orientations. Much of this talk, I believe, is part of the default of intellectual workmen, a revelation of their lack of imagination. As a political type, the conservative, in common with the indifferent, is generally content "to be like other men and to take things as they are," for he believes that the status quo has been built slowly and that as such it is as beneficent an arrangement as can fairly be expected. In brief, and in the consistent extreme, the conservative is a man who abdicates the willful making of history.

The radical (and even the liberal) is a man who does not abdicate. He agrees that many human events, important events at that, may indeed be the results of so many little acts that they are unintended. But he also sees that more and more events in our epoch are not matters of such fate; that they are the results of decisions made and not made by identifiable men who have access to the new means of decision and of power.

Given these means of administration, production, violence, it seems clear that more and more events are due less to any uncontrollable fate than to the decisions, the defaults, the ignorance—as the case may be—of the higher circles of the superstates. To reflect upon the present as history is to understand that history may now be made by default. Understanding that, we no longer need accept as "necessary" the lesser evil. We no longer need to accept historical fate, for fate is a feature of specific kinds of social structure, of irresponsible systems of power. These systems can be changed. Fate can be transcended.

We must come to understand that while the domain of fate is diminishing, the exercise of responsibility is also diminishing and in fact becoming organized as irresponsibility. We must hold men of power variously responsible for pivotal events, and we must unmask their pretensions—and often their own mistaken convictions—that they are not responsible. Our politics, in short, must be the politics of responsibility. Our basic charge against the systems of both the U.S.A. and the U.S.S.R. must be that in differing ways they both live by the politics of irresponsibility.

In East and in West, nowadays, the idea of responsibility is in a sad condition. It is either washed away in liberal rhetoric, or it becomes a trumped-up bloody purge. But we must hold to it; we must be serious about it; we must understand that to use it requires knowledge and inquiry, continual reflection and imagination.

Those who decide should be held responsible to those men and women everywhere who are in any grievous way affected by decisions and defaults. But by whom should they be held responsible? That is the immediate problem of political power. In both East and West today, the immediate answer is: By the intellectual community. Who else but intellectuals are capable of discerning the role in history of explicit history-making decisions? Who else is in a position to understand that now fate itself must be made a political issue?

We must understand that no longer can fate be used either as excuse or as hope, that neither our hopes nor our fears are part of anything inevitable, that we are on our own. Would it not be elementary honesty for the intellectual to realize this new and radical fact of human history and so at least consider the decisions that he is in reality making, rather than to deny by his work that any responsible decisions are open to him?

Democracy requires that those who bear the consequences of decisions have enough knowledge to hold decision-makers accountable. If men hope that contemporary America is to be a democratic society, they must look to the intellectual community for knowledge about those decisions that are now shaping human destiny. Men must depend upon knowledge provided by this community, for by their own private experience they can know only a small portion of the social world that now affects them.

Yet leading intellectual circles in America as elsewhere have not provided true images of the elite as men in irresponsible command of unprecedented means of power. Instead, they have invented images of a scatter of reasonable men, overwhelmed by events and doing their best in a difficult situation. By its softening of the political will, the conservative mood of the intellectuals, out of which these images have arisen, enables men to accept public depravity without any private sense of outrage and to give up the central goal of Western humanism, so strongly felt in nineteenth-century American experience: the audacious control by reason of man's fate.

Nowadays, there is much generalized anguish because there were Causes in the thirties but not any more. What all this means, I think, is that in the thirties the Causes were all set up as programs and little intellectual or moral effort was required to pursue them. At present, the social energy to develop such Causes does not seem available.

As a result there is the often-bemoaned dreariness of the recent cultural scene and the obvious international fact of the political default of cultural workmen. This complaint and this default rest upon the unmet need to specify private troubles out of the vague uneasiness of individuals; to make public issues out of indifference and malaise; and to turn uneasiness and indifference themselves into troubles, issues and problems open to inquiry.

Private uneasiness and public indifference, intellectually speaking, rest upon an unawareness both of imperiled values and of that which is imperiling them. The unfulfilled promise of political thinking that is also culturally sensible stems from the failure to assert the values as well as the perils, and the relationship between them. I cannot help but think that this failure represents another instance in the West of the ascendancy of the international hayseed. There is a showdown on socialism, on its very meaning as well as its chances, going on in Eastern Europe, in Russia, in China. There is a showdown on capitalism in Western Europe and in North America. But for those concerned with the politics of culture and the culture of politics, the most important showdown has to do with the problems that lie in the international encounter of the two superstates. This encounter is not only the encounter of two coexisting kinds of political economy; the problems it poses are not only the problems of how the world is to be industrialized. The world encounter is also an encounter of models of human character. For the kinds of human character that are going to prevail are now being selected and formed as ascendant models of the human being in the United States and in Russia. And within both these overdeveloped societies there is coming a showdown on all the modern expectations about what man can *want* to become.

In the American white-collar and professional hierarchies, and in the middle levels of the Soviet "intelligentsia"—in differing ways but often with frightening convergence—we now witness the rise of the cheerful robot, of the technological idiot, of the crackpot realist. All these types embody a common ethos: rationality without reason. The fate of these types and of this ethos, what is done about them and what they do —that is the real, even the ultimate, showdown on "socialism" and on "capitalism" in our time. It is a showdown on what kinds of human being and what kinds of culture are going to become the commanding models of human aspiration. It is an epochal showdown, separating the contemporary period from "the modern age." To make that showdown clear, as it affects every region of the world and every intimate recess of the self, requires a union of political reflection and cultural sensibility of a sort not really known before. It is a union now scarcely available in the Western intellectual community. Perhaps the attempt to achieve it, and to use it well, is the showdown on human culture itself.

ACKNOWLEDGMENTS

The contents of this book were presented in barest outline during March 1958 in Washington, D. C., as the Sidney Hillman Award Lectures at Howard University. Various parts of the book were also presented in lectures delivered during 1957 and 1958 at the University of Copenhagen, Frankfurt University, a Surrey "weekend" of the London School of Economics, the University of Illinois, Ohio State University, an assembly of the United Church of Canada in Toronto, and the First Midwest Conference of the Unitarian Church.

Articles incorporated here in rewritten form appeared in *The Nation* of December 7, 1957, and March 8, 1958, in the *British Journal of Sociology*, March 1958, and in *Partisan Review* (July–August 1952). I wish to thank the editors of these periodicals for their kind permission to use these materials in their present form.

In preparing this book, I have also used ideas contained in previous published books—in particular, *The Power Elite*—extending and adapting them to the problems of war and of peace.

My friends William Miller of Ridgefield, Connecticut, and Harvey Swados of Valley Cottage, New York, have been generous in helping me to clarify ideas.

C. W. M.

ABOUT THE AUTHOR

C. WRIGHT MILLS *is a leading critic of American society, and author of the modern classics* White Collar *(1951) and* The Power Elite *(1956). He writes for many popular as well as scholarly periodicals, and his work has been published in German, Spanish, Japanese, Danish, French, Polish and Italian translations.*

Professor of Sociology at Columbia, he has taught at many universities in Europe and America, conducted research for government agencies, corporations, and labor unions, and lectured before such groups as the American Management Association, the U. S. Air War College, the International Design Conference, and the William Alanson White Institute of Psychiatry in New York City. In March 1958 he delivered the Sidney Hillman Award Lectures in Washington, D. C., and early in 1959 he will give lecture series in Warsaw and in London.